Timber Frame Home Package

Budget, Design, Estimate, and Secure Your Best Price

Download the Timber Frame Estimator App:
https://itunes.apple.com/ca/app/timber-frame-home-estimator/id901984861?mt=8

Copyright © Jobe Leonard 2013

Download the Timber Frame Estimator App:
https://itunes.apple.com/ca/app/timber-frame-home-estimator/id901984861?mt=8

This book is sold subject to the condition that it shall not, by way of trade or otherwise, be lent, resold, hired out, or otherwise circulated without the publisher's prior consent in any form of binding or cover other than that in which it is published and without a similar condition, being imposed on the subsequent publisher.

For information about special discounts, bulk purchases, or autographed editions please contact Jobe Leonard at JobeLeonard@gmail.com

Write to:

Jobe Leonard Books
1511 Mayflower Lane
Dandridge, TN 37725

Or visit:

www.Jobe.ws

Jobe Leonard

ISBN-13: 978-1495996139
ISBN-10: 1495996131

Introduction

Deciding to build a timber frame home is an exciting leap from the ordinary realm of conventional construction. There are many considerations you must take into account for any project's outcome to be successful. A timber frame home is no different. In this book I will display my decade of construction experience working with a worldwide leader in the log and timber frame home industry. I will use this knowledge to show you the ins and outs of a timber frame home construction project.

In my first book, *Study Abroad, The Book of Jobe*, I wrote about living in a foreign country for my senior year of college. It was completely based upon a true story. I originally created the book to help reconnect with the acquaintances I had made while living in the Netherlands. Much to my surprise it sold thousands of copies in a short period of time and gave me the inspiration to write additional books about other subjects I have a great interest and extensive knowledge about.

Some may think that *Study Abroad, The Book of Jobe* is on the complete opposite end of the spectrum from this book. I actually find them quite similar. Deciding to build a timber frame home is exactly like waking up in a foreign land and having to deal with new customs, languages, and cultures. My first book shows the growth from a rookie traveler to an expert world-renowned voyager and author.

My plan is to take you on a similar journey through the inside world of the timber frame home industry and guide you as you design, budget, and build the best project available. You may have woken up today in a world that was filled with unfamiliar products and confusing verbiage. By the end of this book you will have the confidence to face your project head on.

Maybe instead of a log home you are building a timber frame home. This book will suffice, or there is a similar book available specifically for the log home called, *Log Home Package, Budget, Design, Estimate, and Secure Your Best Price*. You may want to pick up a copy, but feel confident for now you have made a good start. This timber frame home centric version will give you a good grasp of industry concepts, terms, and standard procedures. All the worksheets that are in this book can be printed for free at my website www.Jobe.ws . This book is also available in a large print version for easier reading.

Timber Frame Home Package
Design, Budget, Estimate, and Secure Your Best Price

Table of Contents

Chapter 1	What is my Project?	9
Chapter 2	Budget	11
Chapter 3	Foundation Worksheet	15
Chapter 4	Main Floor Worksheet	21
Chapter 5	Second Floor Worksheet	27
Chapter 6	Full House Budget	33
Chapter 7	Land	37
Chapter 8	Needs	45
Chapter 9	Design	55
Chapter 10	Plan Analysis	61
Chapter 11	Beginning Your Design	73
Chapter 12	Master Bedroom	81
Chapter 13	Master Bathroom	85
Chapter 14	Master Closet	89

Download the Timber Frame Estimator App:
https://itunes.apple.com/ca/app/timber-frame-home-estimator/id901984861?mt=8

Chapter 15	Kitchen	93
Chapter 16	Living Room/ Great Room	97
Chapter 17	Dining Room	101
Chapter 18	Half Bathroom	103
Chapter 19	Stairs	107
Chapter 20	Foundation	109
Chapter 21	Second Floor	113
Chapter 22	Second Floor Bathroom	117
Chapter 23	Windows and Doors	119
Chapter 24	Timber Frame Home Company	129
Chapter 25	Timber Frame Styles	133
Chapter 26	How Long has the Timber Frame in Business	135
Chapter 27	Has Your Timber Frame Home Company Suffered a Recent Bankruptcy?	139

Chapter 28	Are the Timbers Pre-cut at the Timber Frame Home Factory?	143
Chapter 29	Will Your Timber Frame Home Company Send a Crew to Install Their Own Timbers?	145
Chapter 30	Timber Frame Home Company Interviews	147
Chapter 31	Timber Frame Home Package Proposals	149
Chapter 32	How I Might Be Able to Help	155
Chapter 33	Life After the Proposal	159
Chapter 34	Your Contractor	161
Chapter 35	Moving Forward	165
Chapter 36	Timber Frame Home Delivery Day	171
Chapter 37	Completion	175

Download the Timber Frame Estimator App:
https://itunes.apple.com/ca/app/timber-frame-home-estimator/id901984861?mt=8

Chapter 1

What is my project?

The first question that needs to be asked of a project is one that will help guide your entire process. Through the first four chapters I am going to help you answer this question by creating four principles that will steer your project. Your Budget, Needs, Land, and Design are the four major items that will have the most bearing on your timber frame home kit or package. We will review these items in depth before ever speaking to a timber frame home company.

If at anytime these four principles are taken for granted the entire project could begin to crash in a tailspin. It sounds bad, and it really can be. For the thousands of unknowing buyers who purchase timber frame home packages each year it is always a real possibility. Luckily for you, I am going to take you by the hand, and guide you through the best practices and steps to take when creating your *Timber frame Home Package*.

By the end of the book you will know more about a timber frame home kit or package than most project managers working in today's timber frame home industry. Plus you will have a full grasp of your project's

Download the Timber Frame Estimator App:
https://itunes.apple.com/ca/app/timber-frame-home-estimator/id901984861?mt=8

scope and essential details before ever placing the first call to a timber frame home company.

Chapter 2

Budget

The budget of the project is the driving force and will move your project along. It is impossible to build a home that uses $300,000 worth of materials and labor for $200,000. That sounds logical right?

The old adage your grandfather told you, "You get what you pay for," is still true today. However, I will show you how to lower the initial costs of your timber frame home package. This guarantees you get the highest quality materials, best installation services, and spend the least amount of money. All this will happen from the start. Does this sound too good to be true? Read on.

Establishing what can be afforded is paramount. This concept is as simple as the paycheck you expect after a week of your own labor at a daily job. Everyone involved in your project will expect to be paid in a timely fashion for managing your materials, labor, permits, plans, and construction. These project participants must be paid with liquid cash. If not, or the sound of your project coming to a screeching halt will be heard all around the neighborhood.

If you have the cash on hand to finish your project then you only must convince

Download the Timber Frame Estimator App:
https://itunes.apple.com/ca/app/timber-frame-home-estimator/id901984861?mt=8

yourself starting the project is feasible. If you will borrow even the slightest percentage to complete the timber frame home you will then invite dozens of others in to the project. Bankers, appraisers, and loan officers all get to add their input. They will begin to scrutinize all aspects of your project, from every angle.

In both cases you must establish a budget. What is the total amount you can afford to spend? I recommend taking this number and deducting 15% right off the top. Most construction experts recommend adding 15% or more to your total number, because you will always "go over budget." I find this approach completely irresponsible.

The 15% that you deduct from your total feasible budget will be set-aside in an easily accessible liquid emergency fund. This will be used for post completion projects, issues, and unforeseen expenses that arise during and after the construction process.

If your total budget comes to $300,000 using the worksheets in this book then before starting you will take a lump sum of $45,000, and place it in an untouchable construction emergency fund. Your total budget would now be $255,000. Everything we do through the rest of this book will guide you to meeting this goal.

By reading this book you have taken the first step to getting the most out of your timber frame home project and using only the funds you chose to allocate.

If you cannot afford to create an emergency construction fund it is plausible that you might not be able to afford to build the project at this time. You can still prepare your plan, budget, and finish the book. I only ask that you hold off on entering any major agreements until you are on a more solid financial footing. Your goal of building should be to enjoy your home with your friends and family. Not to eat cold beans in the corner of a partially finished, unheated structure wishing you had an emergency fund. Just remember I suggested the concept in the second chapter of *Timber frame Home Package* as you gulp down your next spoonful.

    What is a good way to come up with your own preliminary budget number for a home? I recommend a basic exercise. Determining your project's feasibility can best be calculated using a modified cost per square foot workshop that I present to you in the following pages of this book. I will guide you through the foundation, main floor, and second floor of your timber frame home. This will help you establish a preliminary budget for your timber frame home. Answer the questions then calculate the approximate cost per square foot for each level of your home in the following chapters.

    If you are building this home with a partner now is not the time to work on your own. Mention that you are reading the book to your wife, husband, or other construction partner. Then fill out the following pages simultaneously.

    Purchasing an additional copy of the book may be a good idea to make sure everyone is on the same page, with your timber frame home project, right from the start. Also all the worksheets from this book

Download the Timber Frame Estimator App:
https://itunes.apple.com/ca/app/timber-frame-home-estimator/id901984861?mt=8

can be printed for free at my website, www.Jobe.ws.

Download the Timber Frame Estimator App:
https://itunes.apple.com/ca/app/timber-frame-home-estimator/id901984861?mt=8

Chapter 3

Foundation Worksheet

Now let's take a look at the foundation of your timber frame home project. Here are some questions for you and any building partners to consider.

Research your answers as much as possible and if you do not know at this time choose option 3.

Is your land you will build on flat?

1. Completely flat
2. Slight slope
3. Moderate slope
4. Extreme slope
5. Side of a cliff

Your Numerical Score: __2__

Is this home site easily accessible from the nearest street?

1. Driveway is complete with gravel
2. Driveway is visible with dirt road
3. Clear path of undisturbed grass
4. Unknown path with trees and obstacles
5. Bridge or other infrastructure needed

Your Numerical Score: __1__

Timber Frame Home Package
Design, Budget, Estimate, and Secure Your Best Price

17

Does the local building department require the foundation to have an engineering seal or stamp?

1. No
2. Probably Not
3. Maybe
4. Probably So
5. Yes

Your Numerical Score: _2_

Are you building a slab, piers, crawlspace, or a basement for your foundation?

1. Slab
2. Piers
3. Crawlspace
4. Combination of two of the above
5. Basement

Your Numerical Score: _5_

What will your subfloor system be constructed with?

1. Conventional Wood or Lumber
2. Manufactured Glue Laminated Timbers
3. Pre-built floor trusses
4. Heavy Timbers or Timber frame Material
5. Concrete or Steel

Your Numerical Score: _1_

Download the Timber Frame Estimator App:
https://itunes.apple.com/ca/app/timber-frame-home-estimator/id901984861?mt=8

What will your foundation's wall system be made of?

1. No wall (Slab or Piers)
2. Concrete Block
3. Poured Concrete Walls
4. Pre-insulated Foundation System
5. Insulated Concrete forms

Your Numerical Score: _5_

What portion of the foundation area will be finished during construction?

1. 0%
2. 25%
3. 50%
4. 75%
5. 100%

Your Numerical Score: _4_

Calculations:

Add up your total score from the previous questions and place it in the blank. Range: (7-35)

Your Total Numerical Score: _21_

Divide your score by 7

Total Score Divided By 7: _3_
(Round the number up)

Timber Frame Home Package
Design, Budget, Estimate, and Secure Your Best Price

Find your approximation on the scale below.

1. $30-$45
2. $46-$61
3. $62-$77
4. $78-$93
5. $94-$109

Your Price Range: 231

Now take your price range and multiply it by your desired foundation's square footage.

Your Budget Range: 693,000

  To help you with your process I have created a fictional couple, Tom and Eva. They are building a timber frame home in Tennessee. They chose to use *Timber frame Home Package* to help them gain a better understanding of the timber frame home construction process. Tom and Eva are creating worksheets separately. Over the next few chapters we will follow Tom's worksheets as a guide to help you create your own.

For example:

  Tom is building his new timber frame home in Nashville, TN on a lot that is extremely flat **(Numerical Score 1)**. His site is accessible to the nearest road by a driveway that exists but is currently a dirt path **(Numerical Score 2)**. The building

Download the Timber Frame Estimator App:
https://itunes.apple.com/ca/app/timber-frame-home-estimator/id901984861?mt=8

department is flexible on residential structures and as long as a professionally designed set of blueprints is presented they typically require no engineering stamp **(Numerical Score 2).** His needs require a full basement **(Numerical Score 5)** that will have a subfloor built with conventional lumber purchased from his local lumber yard **(Numerical Score 1).** He plans to use a poured concrete wall system **(Numerical Score 3),** and finish ¾ of the basement for additional living space **(Numerical Score 4).**

Tom's worksheet would look like this.

Calculations:

Add up your total score from the previous questions and place it in the blank. Range: (7-35)

Your Total Numerical Score:
1+2+2+5+1+3+4 =   _18_

Divide your score by 7:   **18/7 = 2.57**

Total Score Divided By 7:   2.57 Rounds up to 3

Find your approximation on the scale below.

1. $30-$45
2. $46-$61
3. $62-$77
4. $78-$93
5. $94-$109

Price Range: $62-$77 per square foot

Now Tom and Eva will take their price range and multiply it by their desired foundation's square footage.

Tom has a need for 1,100 square feet in his basement so he takes the $62 and multiplies it by 1,100 for a low range of $68,200. He then takes the $77 and multiplies it by 1,100 for a high range of $84,700.

Foundation Cost Range: $68,200 -$84,700

Before moving on to the next chapter go ahead and calculate your foundation budget range. Then it is time to move onto the main floor.

Download the Timber Frame Estimator App:
https://itunes.apple.com/ca/app/timber-frame-home-estimator/id901984861?mt=8

Chapter 4

Main Floor Worksheet

Now let's take a peak at the main floor of your timber frame home project. Here are some questions for you and any building partners to consider.

Research your answers as much as possible and if you do not know at this time choose option 3.

How many sinks will be on the main floor of your home?

1. 1
2. 2
3. 3
4. 4
5. 5

Your Numerical Score: ____
What percentage of the main floor's roof system will built using conventional construction with no heavy timbers?

1. 100%
2. 75%
3. 50%
4. 25%
5. 0%

Timber Frame Home Package
Design, Budget, Estimate, and Secure Your Best Price

23

What is the primary construction of the main floor's wall system?

1. Conventional Lumber
2. Conventional and Spray Foam
3. Structural Insulated Panels
4. Insulated Concrete Forms
5. Glass

Your Numerical Score: ____

What type of flooring material will make up the largest percentage of the home?

1. Carpet
2. Wood
3. Tile
4. Exotic Hardwood
5. Stone

Your Numerical Score: ____

What is the primary exterior siding?

1. Vinyl
2. Natural Wood
3. Concrete Board
4. Tree Bark

Download the Timber Frame Estimator App:
https://itunes.apple.com/ca/app/timber-frame-home-estimator/id901984861?mt=8

5. Stone

Your Numerical Score: ____

How many fireplaces are on the main floor?

1. 1
2. 2
3. 3
4. 4
5. 5 or more

What is the square footage of exterior porches?

1. 100-200 square feet
2. 201-400 square feet
3. 401-600 square feet
4. 601-800 square feet
5. 800 or more square feet

Your Numerical Score: ____

What is the highest ceiling height on your main floor?

1. 8'
2. 9'
3. 10'
4. 11'
5. 12' or more including vaulted ceilings.

Timber Frame Home Package
Design, Budget, Estimate, and Secure Your Best Price

Your Numerical Score: ____

Calculations:

Add up your total score from the previous questions and place it in the blank. Range: (8-40)

Your Total Numerical Score: ____

Divide your score by 8

Total Score Divided By 8: ____
(Round the number up)

Find your approximation on the scale below.

1. $100-$125
2. $125-$150
3. $150-$175
4. $175-$200
5. $225 -$250

Your Price Range: ____

Now take your price range and multiply it by your desired foundation's square footage.

Your Budget Range: ____

Let's take a look at how Tom and Eva are progressing with their own main floor budget numbers, worksheets, and project.

Download the Timber Frame Estimator App:
https://itunes.apple.com/ca/app/timber-frame-home-estimator/id901984861?mt=8

For example:

Tom's retirement home has a main floor that is going to have 3 sinks **(Numerical Score 3)**. His roof system is going to be primarily timber frame, but a portion of the master and laundry room will be built only out of conventional lumber **(Numerical Score 3)**. He has chosen carpet for the vast majority of the structure excluding the kitchen and baths **(Numerical Score 1)**. The home's walls are primarily built with structural insulated panels **(Numerical Score 3)**. The primary exterior siding on the main floor is going to be timber frame as well **(Numerical Score 4)**. He has decided against having a fireplace **(Numerical Score 1)**, and has 200 sq. ft of decks and porches **(Numerical Score 2)**. His highest ceiling is a vaulted ceiling in the great room that is open to above and is approximately 22' **(Numerical Score 5)**.

Tom's worksheet would look like this.

Calculations:

Add up your total score from the previous questions and place it in the blank. Range: (8-40)

Total Numerical Score: 3+3+1+3+4+1+2+5 = _22_

Divide your score by 8:   22/8 = 2.75

Numerical Score Divided By 8:   2.75 **Rounds up to 3**

Find your approximation on the scale below.

1. $100-$125
2. $125-$150
3. **$150-$175**
4. $175-$200
5. $225-$250

Numerical Score: $150-$175 per square foot

    Now take your price range and multiply it by your main floor's square footage.

    Tom has estimated he will need for 1,100 square feet on his main floor so he takes the $150 and multiplies it by 1,100 for a low range of $165,000. He then takes the $175 and multiplies it by 1,100 for a high range of $192,500.

Main Floor Cost Range: $165,000 -$192,500

    Before moving on to the next chapter go ahead and calculate your main floor budget range. Then it is time to move onto the second floor.

Download the Timber Frame Estimator App:
https://itunes.apple.com/ca/app/timber-frame-home-estimator/id901984861?mt=8

Chapter 5

Second Floor Worksheet

It is now time to create budget numbers for the second floor of your timber frame home project. Here are some questions for you and any building partners to consider. If you do not have a second floor or loft you can skip this section entirely.

Research your answers as much as possible and if you do not know at this time choose option 3.

What percentage of your second floor plan is a loft that is open to below?

1. 80%
2. 60%
3. 40%
4. 20%
5. 0%

Timber Frame Home Package
Design, Budget, Estimate, and Secure Your Best Price

Your Numerical Score: ____

What type of siding is on the gable ends?

1. Vinyl
2. Natural wood
3. Concrete board siding
4. Tree bark
5. Stone

Your Numerical Score: ____

How many fireplaces are on this floor of the house?

1. 0
2. 1
3. 2
4. 3
5. 4 or more

Your Numerical Score: ____

What is the square footage of the exterior decks, balconies, or porches originating on the second floor?

1. 100-200 square feet
2. 201-400 square feet
3. 401-600 square feet

Download the Timber Frame Estimator App:
https://itunes.apple.com/ca/app/timber-frame-home-estimator/id901984861?mt=8

4. 601-800 square feet
5. 800 or more square feet

Your Numerical Score: ____

How many sinks are on the second floor?

1. 0
2. 1
3. 2
4. 3
5. 4 or more

Your Numerical Score: ____

What type of construction is used to build the exterior walls of the second floor?

1. Conventional Lumber
2. Conventional and Spray Foam
3. Structural Insulated Panels
4. Insulated Concrete Forms
5. Glass

Your Numerical Score: ____

Primary choice of flooring for the second floor?

1. Carpet
2. Wood
3. Tile

Timber Frame Home Package
Design, Budget, Estimate, and Secure Your Best Price

4. Exotic Hardwood
5. Stone

Your Numerical Score: ____

What type of material will be used for your finished roof?

1. 25 year shingle
2. 35 year shingle
3. Metal
4. 50 year architectural shingle
5. Natural Slate or Cedar Shake

Your Numerical Score: ____

Calculations:

Add up your total score from the previous questions and place it in the blank. Range: (8-40)

Your Total Numerical Score:
____

Divide your score by 8

Total Score Divided By 8: ____
(Round the number up)

Find your approximation on the scale below.

1. $80-$105
2. $105-$130

Download the Timber Frame Estimator App:
https://itunes.apple.com/ca/app/timber-frame-home-estimator/id901984861?mt=8

3. $130-$155
4. $155-$180
5. $180-$205

Your Numerical Score: ____

Now take your price range and multiply it by your desired second floor square footage.

Your Budget Range: ____

Tom and Eva are moving along with their budget numbers as well. We can see what they are doing with their second floor to give us a guide to how their home and budget is shaping up.

For Example:

    Tom's upper level of his home is going to be a sleeping loft. It is mainly for his grandchildren. 80% of the floor area is going to be a loft that is open to below **(Numerical Score 1)**. The exterior siding is a vinyl cedar shake **(Numerical Score 1)**. He has no fireplaces **(Numerical Score 1)** or porches **(Numerical Score 1)**. He does include a half bath with one sink for convenience **(Numerical Score 2)**. His gable ends and shed dormer are both built using conventional lumber **(Numerical Score 1)**. For his flooring he decided to use an exotic hardwood he found a small batch of at local supplier **(Numerical Score 4)**. To finish his roof he has chosen a metal roof from the local building supply **(Numerical Score 3)**.

Tom's second floor worksheet would look like this.

Calculations:

Add up your total score from the previous questions and place it in the blank. Range: (8-40)

Total Numerical Score: 1+1+1+1+2+1+4+3= _14_

Divide your score by 8: **14/8 = 1.8**

Numerical Score: **1.8 rounds up to 2**

Find your approximation on the scale below.

1. $80-$105
2. **$105-$130**
3. $130-$155
4. $155-$180
5. $180- $205

Numerical Score: $105-$135 per square foot

Tom has estimated he will need for 200 square feet on his second floor to accommodate his 2 grandkids, a bunkbed and a ½ bath. He takes the $105 and multiplies it by 200 for a low range of $21,000. He then takes the $135 and multiplies it by 200 for a high range of $27,000.

Second Floor Cost Range: $21,000 - $27,000

Download the Timber Frame Estimator App:
https://itunes.apple.com/ca/app/timber-frame-home-estimator/id901984861?mt=8

Now take your price range and multiply it by your second floor's square footage.

Chapter 6

Full House Budget

Now we can take all the numbers and compile a high and low range for our basic preliminary budget. Tom's would look like this

                Low Budget   High Budget

Foundation: $68,200 - $ 94,700

+

Main Floor: $165,000 - $192,500

+

Second Floor: $21,000 - $ 27,000

=

Low Budget Range: $254,200

High Budget Range $314,200
Now let's calculate your budget numbers

Timber Frame Home Package
Design, Budget, Estimate, and Secure Your Best Price

Take your previous numbers and compile a high and low range for our basic preliminary budget.

Low budget   High Budget

Foundation: $_____ - $_____

+

Main Floor: $_____- $_____

+

Second Floor: $_____- $_____

=

Low Budget Range: $_____

High Budget Range $_____

    Now we have a range of numbers to help guide us towards the completion of your timber frame home. This is a great exercise for multiple partners on a project. For instance, a husband and a wife should each complete the checklist in isolation. You may

Download the Timber Frame Estimator App:
https://itunes.apple.com/ca/app/timber-frame-home-estimator/id901984861?mt=8

need two copies of the book or you can print all the worksheets for free from my website at www.Jobe.ws .

Then come together over morning coffee or lunch and begin to compare each of your finish expectations regarding materials and anticipated budget. Next continue to refine your expectations and worksheets to a point you both can agree on before hiring any other team member to assist with your project. You already have the manager of the 2012 National Timber frame Home of The Year helping you through the process so keep reading.

Also take a look at the big picture surrounding your timber frame home project and your current cash position.

In Tom's example he will need a 15% building emergency fund that I prescribed in the beginning. We take his high budget range of $314,200 and multiply that by 15% and find that he would need $47,130 in emergency funds. Now subtract that from the high range and the budget for his project narrows to an easy to understand $254,200 to $267,070.

What is your budget range? I suggest holding this number close to the chest. Use it to guide your entire project in privacy. Just as you do not walk on the used car lot and announce what you want to spend, nor should you do this with your timber frame home company or any other construction team members. Many timber frame home representatives will recommend that you tell them your total budget. Just remember that they are used to working with clients without the inside knowledge that you possess from reading this book. By the time you actually contact your first timber frame home company odds are you may know as much or more about the process than your project manager or salesman himself. So calculate your budget number, remember it, and let's proceed on with the project.

Download the Timber Frame Estimator App:
https://itunes.apple.com/ca/app/timber-frame-home-estimator/id901984861?mt=8

Chapter 7

Land

When reviewing your project's feasibility I made the hasty assumption that you already had that perfect piece of land to place your timber frame home upon. This is the second most important item when constructing your timber frame home. If you have not purchased a piece of land moving forward with the purchase of a timber frame home package or kit is like eating a box of donuts while running on the treadmill. You are wasting your time.

Any quality timber frame home manufacturer will offer to walk the land with you before you buy their timber frame package. Some limitations regarding a pre-sale land inspection may involve complications caused by great distances. For example, I shipped a timber frame home to San Bernardino, California and the timber frame home company I work for is in

Tennessee. In an instance like this it might be better for the timber frame home representative to make a visit to your land after the project has been shipped. This ensures that the client is happy with the project and received what they expected. I would never recommend punishing a timber frame home company for using common sense on your project.

On the same note, if a site visit was needed to make the sale of a timber frame package to a client, I would have traveled anywhere on behalf of my company. However, a commitment to visit a site typically involves a client that is much further along in the process than we are right now. To get the most out of your timber frame home representative you should schedule the site visit when you are within 30 days of the purchase of your timber frame home package. With a local supplier they may be able to walk your lot with you before you purchase the land. This is less common, but might be worth asking. The worst they can tell you is, "No".

What type of land will you build on? I am certain you already have an idea of this in your head, or maybe the land is already in your family or your possession. Maybe you just need to finalize a divorce from fighting over the finishes and budget numbers from the previous chapters of this book. Just kidding, of course.

A real estate professional can point you in the right direction, but first you need to know what area of the country. Narrow this down with your partner. Start with which

Download the Timber Frame Estimator App:
https://itunes.apple.com/ca/app/timber-frame-home-estimator/id901984861?mt=8

state you will build in and then progress to a smaller area like a region, county, or city. Again teamwork is key on a multi-person project. Deciding on an area that all parties can agree on will guard your project from having a key member withdrawal support during the most important phases.

Keep in mind that the previous budget we created may be met with extreme enthusiasm in some parts of the country. There are other areas where you may be laughed at. Building a timber frame home takes tough skin. With this book, and the resources it provides, it will ensure that you will have the last and longest laugh.

I suggest asking your real estate professional what the typical building cost are in the area and see if they mesh with what we have come up with so far. If not, there are multiple locations within a real estate agent's territory. They might be able to point you closer to the correct piece of land and building market.

One of the many positives of building a timber frame home and purchasing a timber frame home package is that it can act as a large price equalizer for the project. Imagine that you found your land in a bustling oil town in North Dakota. However, due to a labor shortage, even an employee at McDonald's starts at $18.00 per hour. This drives up the cost of construction services up in the area. This is because flipping burgers is now more lucrative than hammering nails. To entice quality help you need a higher rate to attract workers. Plus the wages and opportunities for skilled construction workers are obviously very high. This is because oil companies are also competing for this type of laborer.

In this instance, the low labor rates from a timber frame home company from a state like Tennessee begin to make a lot of sense. The reasons why lie in the fact that a large majority of the project can be manufactured and installed using a labor force from a lower wage market. These Tennessee labor rates can bypass the pain of the inflated North Dakota rates. This is just one example. I am sure you can think of a town or location within 30 minutes of where you live that has a higher cost of living, real estate value, or labor rates than another location in the surrounding area.

Another instance where land is a driving force is in the instance of a planned development. There are many advantages and disadvantages of building in these properties. I like to think of it as "Brand Name Land." Someone has given a group of properties a name, an identity, and organized a group of collective owners to manage and oversee the property after the initial inception.

The advantages of building at these properties are that they are usually filled with amenities like the following:

-Gated Entrances
-Club Houses
-Neighborhood Boat Ramps
-Community Equestrian Facilities
-Utilities like Electric, Water, Sewer

I am sure you can name a few more.

Download the Timber Frame Estimator App:
https://itunes.apple.com/ca/app/timber-frame-home-estimator/id901984861?mt=8

Some of the disadvantages of building in these developments would be:

-Homeowner's fees
-Covenants
-Restrictions
-Architectural Review Committees
-Inflated Initial Land Costs

You could probably name a few more disadvantages as well.

Just be weary when building a timber frame home. Make sure the restrictions allow the construction of a timber frame or timber home. Even if the covenants and bylaws do not explicitly prohibit the construction there may be an architectural review committee.

These committees can be to your advantage. They maintain construction standards and keep resale values up. However, what if the people who make up the board have poor architectural taste or personal vendettas against timber frame homes in general? If you purchased land in this development and just purchased your timber frame home kit then you may be in for a major surprise. Imagine that the architectural review committee rejects your plan. You are now at the neighborhood prude club's mercy. It happens.

When choosing your land there are many things to consider with your timber frame home and which piece of land is right for your project. If you look hard enough you can find a reason to hate or love any piece of property. With construction costs and real estate purchases I am a supporter of the belief that you should stay within a budget. You must make sure you know what your land budget is well before shopping for real estate. Never buy a piece of land you cannot afford.

There is absolutely zero reason to buy a piece of land that pushes your project back until you are 85 years old, because you overspent on a piece of ground. By that time the odds that you will be able enjoy your new timber frame home are very slim and the budget numbers from this book will have probably doubled due to inflation and increasing material costs.

Also remember that it is a good idea to pay back any money that has been loaned on your land before you build. The bank may not come right out and say it, but they will penalize you if you owe too much or paid too much for the property. If you are a cash buyer, the only person you have to please is yourself.

Be reasonable when buying that magical piece of property. Do not expect it to increase in value. If it does, it is a nice bonus. I realize that everyone, since you were a kid, has told you, "Land, they are never making any more of it." Well that is true, but when you drive through the most populated states in our country there are thousands of acres of undeveloped land.

Someone may own the property now, but they will not live forever. There will always be greedy grandchildren who care only about putting cash in their pockets. As soon as the casket is closed, they will place the family piece of land on the market. The piece of real estate that would never be "made" again is

Download the Timber Frame Estimator App:
https://itunes.apple.com/ca/app/timber-frame-home-estimator/id901984861?mt=8

suddenly available once more. While they may not make any more land, there is always land available.

Also realize that there are hundreds of properties in every state that were purchased to be built on and never will be. I have seen this first hand. Over 80% of landowners in specific areas are from other states. Out of state speculators purchased the properties in the early 2000's and expected to make a quick profit by flipping the property for twice what they paid. They still may, but I would advise you stay away from land for the strict purpose of turning a profit while undertaking your timber frame home project.

Do not fall into the speculative land money trap. This wide open pit is full of others who are paying HOA fees, property taxes, lot mowing crews, and many additional everyday expenditures on land that will never built on or enjoyed. Stay the course for the timber frame home we are slowly creating, and you will be greatly rewarded. If you want to buy real estate and make loads of money take a break from reading and play a game of Monopoly with your construction partner. Someone always loses. Then get back to your timber frame home project.

If you start with a feasible plan, emergency fund, and a doable budget, the project of your dreams is within your reach. If you constantly stretch and over reach you will be left with a sore pocket book and bitter feelings. You took the correct first step of reading this guide so get out there and find your perfect lot. That is if you do not own it already.

Download the Timber Frame Estimator App:
https://itunes.apple.com/ca/app/timber-frame-home-estimator/id901984861?mt=8

Chapter 8

Needs

You took my budget test in the beginning of the book. Then you spoke about your land needs in the last chapter. If you are still moving forward with your timber frame home project, then there is probably something to it.

Now let's talk about your needs. Your budget pages created a great guide for starting conversations about your needs. Chances are, without much painful thought or argument you were able to fill out the entire checklist.

If you are working on this project with a partner then go ahead and grab your checklists from Chapters 3 through 5. Fill out the corresponding pages to find out what portions of the project you both already agree on. If it is just you building the project then this exercise will be easy. You just need to make sure you adhere to your budget and stick to your choices from your budget worksheet.

Foundation

Enter corresponding numerical values from budget worksheet

	You	Partner
Land		
Engineering		
Slab/Crawlspace/Basement		
Subfloor Joist		
Foundation Wall		
Finished Basement Percentage		
Foundation Budget Average	_____	_____

Download the Timber Frame Estimator App:
https://itunes.apple.com/ca/app/timber-frame-home-estimator/id901984861?mt=8

Main Floor

Enter corresponding numerical values from budget worksheet

Percentage of Conventional Construction

Wall System Construction

Flooring

Siding

Porches

Ceiling

Main Floor Budget Average   _____   _____

Second Floor

Loft Area Percentage

Exterior Siding

Fireplaces

Porches

Sinks

Wall System

Flooring Material

Roof Finish

Second Floor Budget Average _____ _____

  Now let's take a look at how Tom and his wife Eva's worksheets turned out. Then I will show you how to analyze the information you have so far.

Tom's Need Comparrison
Foundation

Enter corresponding numerical values from budget worksheet

	Tom	Eva
Land	1	1
Driveway/Accessibility	2	2
Engineering	2	3
Slab/Crawlspace/Basement	5	5
Subfloor Joist	1	5
Foundation Wall	3	2

Download the Timber Frame Estimator App:
https://itunes.apple.com/ca/app/timber-frame-home-estimator/id901984861?mt=8

Finished Basement Percentage   4   3

Foundation Budget Average   __3__   __3__

    When we analyze this section, we see that all the categories are relatively similar. The most important agreeable point, the budget, is identical. One glaring difference is the subfloor joist material. After Tom spoke with his wife about this section of the home, they realized that her answer of 5 was caused by confusion about the actual material. She assumed a timber frame home would need a heavy timber subfloor, but quickly agreed that the more common conventional subfloor would suffice for the basement area.

    Compromise like this should be common as we move from this portion on. Overall the numbers are close enough and the similarities in the two worksheets are many. We can feel comfortable that parties understand the foundation portion of the home and are in agreement on more than a majority of the major items. Now let's look at the main floor of the home.

Main Floor

Enter corresponding numerical values from budget worksheet

	Tom	Eva
Sinks	3	3
Percentage Conventional Construction	3	2
Wall System Construction	3	3

	Tom	Eva
Flooring	1	2
Siding	4	4
Fireplaces	1	2
Porches	2	3
Ceiling	5	5
Main Floor Budget Average	__3__	__3__

    Upon reviewing this section it is promising to see that the budget is still very similar. Any major discrepancies need to be further investigated. After discussing the differences in some of their numbers, Tom agreed that carpet was probably not the best choice for a cabin style home. He and Eva now plan to go with his wife's choice of wood flooring.

    On the porches they resolved to take a closer look in the next chapter of the book when they begin the actual design of the home. They also talked about a fireplace. Due to the fact that a wood burning fireplace can be a major expense they agreed to investigate it further. For now they are not going to pursue one. The major items of the main floor are in agreement thus far. Now they move on to the second floor of the home, and so should you.

Second Floor

	Tom	Eva
Loft Area Percentage	1	2

Download the Timber Frame Estimator App:
https://itunes.apple.com/ca/app/timber-frame-home-estimator/id901984861?mt=8

Exterior Siding	1	3
Fireplaces	1	1
Porches	1	1
Sinks	1	1
Wall System	1	3
Flooring Material	4	2
Roof Finish	3	5
Second Floor Budget Average	_2_	_2_

    This section's results were very similar in regards to budget, but when we take a closer look we realize that a few key areas have differences.

    Eva wants a larger loft area, full timber frame gables, wood floors, and a cedar shake roof. Tom has created his budget sheet looking for a smaller loft, vinyl shake gables, a conventionally built gable system and a metal roof. They both agree that nothing on the list is a deal breaker. From the information they have, they can see that they both like the cedar shake look. Tom has the shake look on the gable. Eva has them on the roof. A compromise can be found.

    One of them wants an exotic hardwood and the other would like a regular milled hardwood. This is another easy compromise. They both like the look of a wood floor. This is a decision that can be made later in the project when they see how their plan progresses.

    The one major area of disagreement is on the full timber frame gables. Tom wants to conventionally build them, and his wife would like them to be made of full timber frames. They agree to move ahead and research the area further as they move through the prescribed processes in the book.

    Now take a look at both of your budget checklist floor by floor. If your budgets are similar then there is hope. If you see more than six extremely large contrasts, or your budgets on a single floor are off by more than two numerical values this is something you will need to work out with your construction partner. Do this before moving onto the design stage. Remember we are laying out the most important aspects of the project. The more we can agree on and understand now the smoother the entire process will go.

    Also double-check to make sure the major contrast scores are not because of indifference or misunderstanding. On the first day of a timber frame project, many people (including me) would fail to understand exactly what a subfloor joist system is, or what is the proper material to use. This provides a good opportunity to educate yourself further and talk as a team to make sure the base of your project is on solid ground.

    So what does the checklist tell us? All the number values that are identical are items that are already agreed upon. You can go ahead place them on your need list. This is assuming your budget and emergency savings numbers are still feasible. Any items that have a slightly differing score can be talked through and negotiated. Perhaps on items that are similar like Tom's and Eva's cedar shakes and flooring there is a common ground.

    See what you can find compromise on. Working as a team will be important throughout the entire process. You need to perfect the decision making process now before you invite anyone else into the project.

Download the Timber Frame Estimator App:
https://itunes.apple.com/ca/app/timber-frame-home-estimator/id901984861?mt=8

Another item that you already know is the number of sinks. This number will tell you the amount of bathrooms. All you need to do is subtract one from the total number of sinks. That is your number of bathrooms. The only exception would be if you have a laundry sink or more than one kitchen.

Let's take what we know and place it in the worksheet below as you begin to form your need list.

Number of Bathrooms :
Number of Bedrooms:
Foundation Square Footage:
Main Floor Square Footage:
Porch and Deck Square Footage:
Flooring:
Wall System:
Fireplaces:

Here is an example of Tom and Eva's Need skeleton at this point in the process:

Number of Bathrooms: 1 Full 2 Halfs
Number of Bedrooms: 2
Foundation Square Footage: 1,100
Main Floor Square Footage: 1,100
Second Floor Square Footage: 200
Porch Square Footage: 200-600
Flooring: Wood
Wall System: Structural Insulated
               Panels
Fireplaces: None

This makes up your basic set of needs. Armed with this, your land, and your budget you are ready to start designing your own

Timber Frame Home Package
Design, Budget, Estimate, and Secure Your Best Price

plan, find an existing plan, or hire someone to design a plan for you. We will be constantly adding to this sheet throughout the design phase we are about to begin. Be sure to keep your need list handy. The need list and other worksheets can all be printed free of charge from www.Jobe.ws.

Download the Timber Frame Estimator App:
https://itunes.apple.com/ca/app/timber-frame-home-estimator/id901984861?mt=8

Chapter 9

Design

Most "experts" will disagree with my methods of beginning with the budget first before asking you to create a basic floor plan. My method is based on building a pathway to communication of partners involved in the project. This allows the whole project to be budget minded. Before you ever touch the first piece of pencil lead to paper, you know your goal, your needs, and understand the importance of the right piece of land in the best location.

When working with timber frame home customers on the purchase of timber frame home package, if your representative does not try to gauge the size of your project before throwing designs at you they are extremely under qualified. Imagine if you went to the tailor to buy new pants and the store clerk never wrapped a measuring tape around your waist. His advice to you was to stroll around the department and try on as many untagged pants as possible. Surely you would find a pair that fits, but at what expense?

Would you be so worn out at the end of the process that you simply bought the first pair that fits? Or would you fall into the other extreme and never buy a pair pants. The frustration of trying on so many different pairs and finding them much to large,

Download the Timber Frame Estimator App:
https://itunes.apple.com/ca/app/timber-frame-home-estimator/id901984861?mt=8

followed by much too small would be too much.

The approach we followed from the first chapter was to gauge your project's pants size. Now you can mosey around a timber frame home company's design department and try on the pants (plans) that fit your project instead of frustrating yourself to the point of giving up by going in the wrong direction multiple times.

Who will design your timber frame home? Most timber frame home companies worth buying a package from will be able to create a set of blueprints for you. These plans will meet your area's building codes, project needs, and most importantly your budget. If they cannot, then why are you interested in hiring them to build the most important structural portion of your home? The reason I recommend having your plans drawn by the same company that designs your timber system is threefold.

First, all modern plans are copyrighted. The penalties for violations are stiff. If you want to steal someone's intellectual property then you should go ahead and triple your emergency construction budget. There are law firms all over the world that make a living off enforcing copyright infringements. Do not steal someone's plans. You should also immediately question the integrity of a company that will infringe a competitor's copyright to earn your business. What if the resulting lawsuit bankrupts the timber frame company in the middle of your project after you have placed a large deposit?

Second, the timber frame home company will have to design a set of plans for your specific timber frame system. God bless the folks that put in a foundation according to what they think will work. Then they try to order the timber frame system. It is a recipe for disaster. You and any future buyer will spend a lifetime paying for this mistake.

The other end of the spectrum is hiring architects and engineers to design the timber portions of the home. These can turn out to be the most expensive projects. This happens when an uncompromising structural design office has required a size of timber that does not exist or is simply the wrong one for the job. Even though an independent design firm can be very helpful on a home construction project, many times they have little clue as to the industry design standards for a timber frame home. This includes the proper species, timber sizing, strengths, moisture content, and cuts that can be made.

The third reason you should allow the company you choose to design your plans is that a quality timber frame home company will install what they sell with factory trained representatives. An architect will never lift a hammer on your site unless it is to smash open your piggy bank to design in one more Feng Shui water fountain for your living room. The same is true with an engineer. They would not lift a hammer because the handle they designed for it would be so thick and over compensated for that they could never wrap their hand around it.

Of course, I am joking, and I have worked with plenty of fantastic architects and engineers. The more people you involve in the design process the more it will cost you. It is

Download the Timber Frame Estimator App:
https://itunes.apple.com/ca/app/timber-frame-home-estimator/id901984861?mt=8

as simple as that. Work completed on your project demands a paycheck. We have recognized this concept from the very beginning. I am looking out for your budget first and foremost and the less people you place on the payroll the better at this point.

After all is said and done your budget is your most important aspect. If you choose a quality timber frame package manufacturer (I will show you how), your entire project will be protected and the design process will be a breeze.

You should let the timber frame home company manage the design process. This will lower your initial budget on the front end by designing the best, most structurally sound options into your home from the beginning.

If after choosing this quality timber frame home company, a need arises for engineering or an architectural review then allow the timber frame company to hire one on your behalf. They typically know the firms that best understand their timber frame products and services. They can make the process of dealing with outside design firms much less tedious. After all, you do not want to go shopping for your pre-sized pants at the neighborhood tire store.

Where can you find designs? If you are building a 100-5,000 square foot home odds are that someone has already built something similar. Look in magazines, shop for books, and search your favorite timber frame manufacturer's websites. Also I suggest that during this process that you and your partner draw as many of the basic floor plans as you can on your own.

Timber Frame Home Package
Design, Budget, Estimate, and Secure Your Best Price

If you see something you like most companies can provide a free design catalog. Just be weary initially to give too much information about your project. As part of my training, when I started in the timber frame home industry, I was given a similar task. I had to nail down a design and shop the industry to see what was available and what each competing company had to offer. 10 years later I still get postcards, phone calls, and mailings. There are dedicated sales forces working for timber frame home manufacturers. I will eventually guide you to them when the time is right. If you call them now they will set their sights on you for the next decade. Especially if you pump one of the their salesmen up with some juicy information on your project too early. The time will come to contact them for pricing, but not quite yet.

If I were brand new and starting a project this design guide in the following chapters, is exactly how I would handle it. I suggest that during this process that you and your partner draw as many of the basic floor plans as you can on your own.

With your budget and needs list in mind it is now time to locate or create five plans as a team that meet those needs. These can come from books, the Internet, or design websites. However, the five plans you choose should include at least one floor plan sketch from each of the partners involved with the project. I have worked through this process with many of my clients. This includes a design I worked on that won the 2012 National Timber Home of the Year Award.

Download the Timber Frame Estimator App:
https://itunes.apple.com/ca/app/timber-frame-home-estimator/id901984861?mt=8

Chapter 10

Plan Analysis

After locating and creating your 5 basic plans. Start communicating again with your partner and make 2 copies of each of the 5 plans. These should be plans that you both have picked and designed. In private have each partner involved in the process rank each plan from 1-5 and list 2 negatives and 2 positives from each plan. Keep your negatives and positives to simple 2 and 3 word descriptive statements. Then fill out the form below.

<u>Negatives   Positives   Plan Rank</u>
Plan 1

Plan 2

Plan 3

Plan 4

Plan 5

<u>Plan Rank Plan Average   Top Plan</u>
Plan 1

Plan 2

Download the Timber Frame Estimator App:
https://itunes.apple.com/ca/app/timber-frame-home-estimator/id901984861?mt=8

Plan 3

Plan 4

Plan 5

Now sit down once more over a cup of tea or breakfast and talk about your rankings of each plan. Pay close attention to which plans you both afforded high ranks. Again using averages calculate your top 3 plans according to your plan analysis rankings. These 3 plans will move to the top of your list and on to the next step in your design process.

Also review your lists of negatives and positives for each of the plans and pay close attention to emerging patterns. Both of you may have mentioned a main floor master bedroom or an open kitchen. These will be features you liked on several different plans. It is ok to go ahead and transfer this information over to your need list.

Using the same eye for detail you should also make note of which negatives form a common theme on the list. Knowing your likes and dislikes will be powerful knowledge for you as we move through the basic design process, into timber frame package negotiations, and through the construction process. Now based on ranking take the average ranking of each plan and move your top 3 on to the next round of your design.

See Tom's and his wife's example of their top 5 plans:

Timber Frame Home Package
Design, Budget, Estimate, and Secure Your Best Price

Plan 1 Details:

Second Floor

Stairs 4'x15'
Loft: 16'x21'
Half Bath: 8'x10'
Square Feet: 336

Main Floor

Master Bedroom: 16'x15'
Master Bathroom: 8'x13'
Master Closet: 3'x7'
Kitchen: 12'x12'
Dining: 17'x8'
Living Room: 20'x12'
Half Bath: 7'x7'
Square Feet: 990

Foundation

Utility Room: 10'x12'
Square Feet: 990

Total Square Footage: 2,316

Download the Timber Frame Estimator

https://itunes.apple.com/ca/app/timber-frame-home-estimator/id901984861?mt=8

Plan 2 Details:

Second Floor

Stairs 4'x15'
Loft: 24'x8'
Half Bath: None
Square Feet: 192

Main Floor

Master Bedroom: 12'x14'
Master Bathroom: 6'x16'
Master Closet: 4'x16'
Kitchen: 8'x21'
Dining: 6'x9'
Living Room: 10'x30'
Half Bath: 8'x10'
Square Feet: 900

Foundation

Utility Room: 12'x12'
Square Feet: 900

Total Square

Timber Frame Home Package
Design, Budget, Estimate, and Secure Your Best Price

Plan 3 Details:

Second Floor

Stairs 4'x15'
Loft: 10'x25'
Half Bath: 8'x10'
Square Feet: 250

Main Floor

Master Bedroom: 14'x17'
Master Bathroom: 8'x10'
Master Closet: 4'x8'
Kitchen: 10'x17'
Dining: 6'x16'
Great Room: 16'x16'
Half Bath: 8'x10'
Square Feet: 1000

Foundation

Utility Room: 8'x25'
Square Feet: 1000

Total Square Footage: 2250

Download the Timber Frame Estimator

https://itunes.apple.com/ca/app/timber-frame-home-estimator/id901984861?mt=8

Plan 4 Details:

Second Floor

Stairs 4'x15'
Loft: 12'x20'
Half Bath: 12'x7'
Square Feet: 240

Main Floor

Master Bedroom: 12'x15'
Master Bathroom: 9'x12'
Master Closet: 7'x8'
Kitchen: 12'x13'
Dining: 8'x14'
Living Room: 14'x21'
Half Bath: 6'x7'
Square Feet: 999

Foundation

Utility Room: 11'x12'
Square Feet: 999

Total Square Footage: 2,238

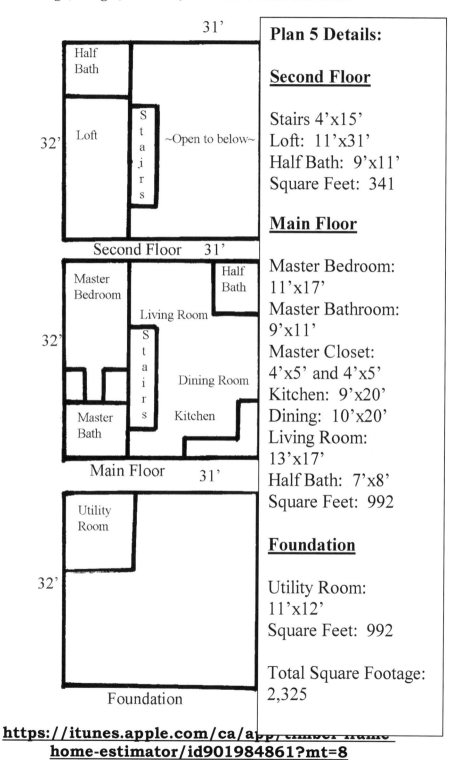

Tom's Plan Analysis

	Negatives	Positives	Plan Rank
Plan 1	Small master closet	Nice loft layout	5
Plan 2	No upstairs bathroom	Big kitchen	4
Plan 3	Utility too large	Master layout	1
Plan 4	Small Dining area	Great Room	2
Plan 5	Small Dining Area	Master suite layout	3

Timber Frame Home Package
Design, Budget, Estimate, and Secure Your Best Price

Eva's Plan Analysis

	Negatives	Positives	Plan Rank
Plan 1	Cramped Master closet	Large Kitchen	4
Plan 2	Small master Bath	Large Dining	3
Plan 3	Master Closet	Loft Layout	2
Plan 4	Kitchen in corner	Master setup	1
Plan 5	Half bathroom placement	Open Kitchen	5

	Plan Rank	Plan Average	Top Plan
Plan 1	(5+4)/2 =	4.5	
Plan 2	(4+3)/2 =	3.5	
Plan 3	(1+2)/2 =	1.5	Yes
Plan 4	(2+1)/2 =	1.5	Yes
Plan 5	(3+5)/2 =	4	Yes

Download the Timber Frame Estimator App:
https://itunes.apple.com/ca/app/timber-frame-home-estimator/id901984861?mt=8

Now after the plan analysis is done we can go back and update our need skeleton to include the items we both found appealing. Tom's new need skeleton would look like this.

Number of Bathrooms: 1 Full 2 Halfs
Number of Bedrooms: 2
Foundation Square Footage: 1,100
Main Floor Square Footage: 1,100
Second Floor Square Footage: 200
Porch Square Footage: 200-600
Flooring: Wood
Wall System: Structural Insulated Panels
Fireplaces: None
Common Positives: Large kitchen, Master Layouts.
Common Negatives: Small Master Closet.

After you have updated your need skeleton and found your top 3 plans it is time to delegate responsibilities. These will carry you through the rest of the project. If you are the only one involved in the construction process then congratulations. You get to do both tasks. If you have a partner then now is the time to decide who will be your project's "Designer" and who will act as your project's "Recorder."

Designer Roles:

Ability to draw squares and lines.
Creativity Leader
Follow needs, budget, and plan analysis.

Recorder Roles:

Keeps notes on design.
Analyze plan changes.
Ensures adherence to budget, needs, and plan analysis.

  Now that you have decided who is going to fill each of these simple roles it is time to gather a few tools to make our advancing design process much easier. The designer will need a pencil, an architectural scale, and pad of graph paper. The recorder will need a notebook, the need skeleton, the budget, the top 3 plans, and a pencil. All the items above can be purchased at any office supply store.
  After you have these materials, it is time to begin your design. This is the easiest and also one of the most important parts of the process. The formation of this team will make working with your timber frame home company in the later chapters of this guide much easier. Also it allows all partners to be involved and have an important role throughout the rest of the process.

Download the Timber Frame Estimator App:
https://itunes.apple.com/ca/app/timber-frame-home-estimator/id901984861?mt=8

Chapter 11

Beginning Your Design

The project's Recorder has a notebook created. They will remove your top three plans. Place the three plans in front of you. Then write out the outside dimensions of the top 3 plans.

Take a look at Tom and Eva's top three plans and follow the example shown on the following pages to create your initial timber frame home footprint.

Timber Frame Home Package
Design, Budget, Estimate, and Secure Your Best Price

Plan 3 Details:

Second Floor

Stairs 4'x15'
Loft: 10'x25'
Half Bath: 8'x10'
Square Feet: 250

Main Floor

Master Bedroom: 14'x17'
Master Bathroom: 8'x10'
Master Closet: 4'x8'
Kitchen: 10'x17'
Dining: 6'x16'
Great Room: 16'x16'
Half Bath: 8'x10'
Square Feet: 1000

Foundation

Utility Room: 8'x25'
Square Feet: 1000

Total Square Footage: 2250

Download the Timber Frame Estimator App:
https://itunes.apple.com/ca/app/timber-frame-home-estimator/id901984861?mt=8

Plan 4 Details:

Second Floor

Stairs 4'x15'
Loft: 12'x20'
Half Bath: 12'x7'
Square Feet: 240

Main Floor

Master Bedroom: 12'x15'
Master Bathroom: 9'x12'
Master Closet: 7'x8'
Kitchen: 12'x13'
Dining: 8'x14'
Living Room: 14'x21'
Half Bath: 6'x7'
Square Feet: 999

Foundation

Utility Room: 11'x12'
Square Feet: 999

Total Square Footage: 2,238

In Tom and Eva's case Tom ⟨ the recorder. From their top grou plans, Plan 2 is 30'x30', Plan 3 is 25'x40', and Plan 4 is 27'x37'. Now the Recorder will make an average of the short wall (30'+25'+37')/3= 30.67'. This rounds up to 31'. Then he will take an average of the long wall (30'+40'+37')/3= 35.67'. This rounds up to 36'. The starting dimension that the Recorder presents to the Designer is 31'x36'.

Eva chose to be the designer. She takes the 31'x36' dimension and transfers it onto 3 pieces of plan graph paper using the scale and pencil. She then takes the bottom of each of the three pages and label one of them **"Second Floor**," **"Main Floor**," and **"Foundation**." Then Eva writes the basic dimension on the top right and left side of all three plans.

Tom and Eva's first plan layout looks like this:

Download the Timber Frame Estimator App:
https://itunes.apple.com/ca/app/timber-frame-home-estimator/id901984861?mt=8

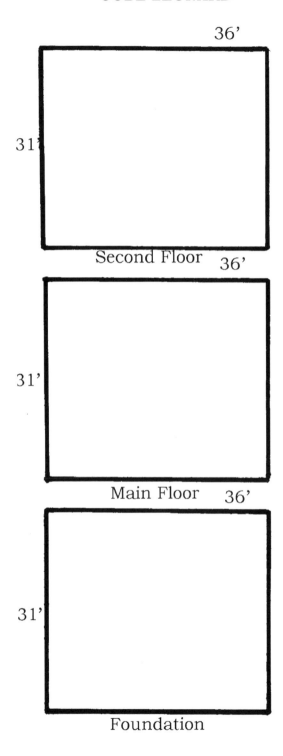

Main Floor Design

Now it is time to create your basic layouts using your average dimensions. If you have had trouble finding a scale thus far or have questions on starting your design send me an e-mail at **JobeLeonard@gmail.com**. I can guide you in the right direction. If you are ready to go to work without the scale or any assistance then use the squares on your graph to represent one foot.

Download the Timber Frame Estimator App:
https://itunes.apple.com/ca/app/timber-frame-home-estimator/id901984861?mt=8

Chapter 12

Master Bedroom

After these layouts are created we are going to move on to the Master Bedroom. The Recorder will dictate any "Positives" or "Negatives" that were discussed during the plan analysis. These will relate to the master bedroom and be noted at the top of the page. Then the dimensions of the Master Bedroom from the top three plans are noted as well. Also indicate whether the Master should be drawn onto the Foundation, Main Floor, or Second Floor layout. Typically it will be on the Main Floor. By now you should know exactly which floor to put it on. If not, review your need list, positives, and negatives.

For Example:

In Tom and Eva's case the dimensions are 12'x14', 12'x17', and 12'x15'. Tom, acting as the Recorder then does a short wall average (12'+12'+12')/3= 12'. Next he does a long wall average (14'+17'+15')/3= 15.33'. This rounds down to 15'. Tom comes up with a room dimension of 12'x15'.
According to their list of positives and negatives, they were both particularly happy with the Master Bedroom in Plan 4 so they agree to orient the Master Bedroom in a similar setting on the main floor.

Download the Timber Frame Estimator App:
https://itunes.apple.com/ca/app/timber-frame-home-estimator/id901984861?mt=8

See Tom & Eva's example on the following page:

Timber Frame Home Package
Design, Budget, Estimate, and Secure Your Best Price

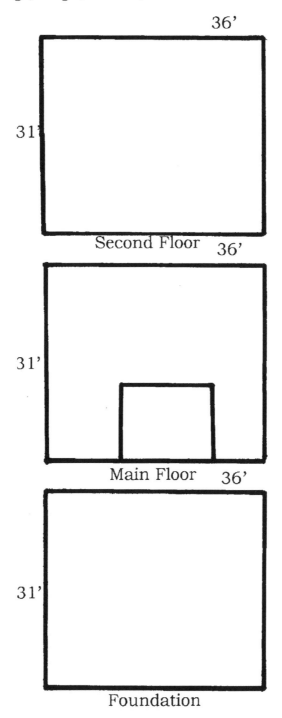

https://itunes.apple.com/ca/app/timber-frame-home-estimator/id901984861?mt=8

The Recorder on your team should now compile dimensions and create the wall length averages. Along with corresponding positives and negatives you listed. Then the designer on your team will sketch the Master Bedroom's dimension onto your plans without worrying about windows, doors, and furniture. Just focus on the placement of the rough dimensions.

Timber Frame Home Package
Design, Budget, Estimate, and Secure Your Best Price

Download the Timber Frame Estimator App:
https://itunes.apple.com/ca/app/timber-frame-home-estimator/id901984861?mt=8

Chapter 13

Master Bathroom

We are now going to show the Master Bathroom on the plan using the same process.

For Example:

Tom and Eva's top three plans have Master Bathroom that is 6'x16', 14'x17', and 12'x15'. Tom calculates the average of the short wall as (6'+14'+12')/3= 10.67' rounded up as 11'. The long wall average is (16'+17'+15')/3 = 16'. The room size for their master bathroom will be 11'x16'.
Tom then lists corresponding positives and negatives corresponding to the Master Bathroom. The most prominent negative they find is that neither of them wanted a cramped Master Bathroom. This was because of the long narrow Master Bathroom on plan 2. The average method of sizing the room has eliminated this issue. They are now left with an 11'x16' Master Bathroom that meets both of their needs. He passes the list to Eva to sketch onto the Main Floor Plan.

Take a look at Tom and Eva's sketch as they sketch their Master Bathroom.

Timber Frame Home Package
Design, Budget, Estimate, and Secure Your Best Price

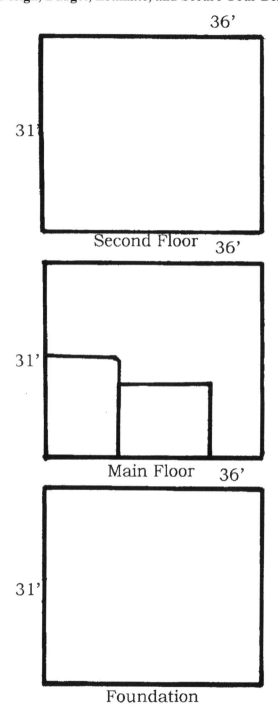

https://itunes.apple.com/ca/app/timber-frame-home-estimator/id901984861?mt=8

Following the example above your team's recorder will compile the size of you master bathroom using the top 3 plans' dimension averages. Then pass these along to the designer to be shown on the applicable page of sketches.

Download the Timber Frame Estimator App:
https://itunes.apple.com/ca/app/timber-frame-home-estimator/id901984861?mt=8

Chapter 14

Master Closet

Next we are going to place the Master Closet into your floor plan using similar reasoning.

For Example:

The plans Tom and Eva are using have master closets that are 4'x6', 4'x8', and 7'x8'. Tom averages the short wall at (4'+4'+7')/3= 5'. Then he does a long wall average of (6'+8'+8')/3= 7.33' which rounds down to 7'. Using short and long wall averages Tom computes a size of 5'x7' for the closet walls.
He reviews the plan analysis and lists the applicable positives and negatives. He finds a common theme of disliking narrow, small, and cramped closets. The 5'x7' average is still a bit small, but they decide to see how the rest of the home lays out, and if they have any additional space they will use it there. Tom passes the information over to Eva. She then pencils the closet space onto the main floor plan. The main floor plan with the master closet added can be seen on the next page.

Timber Frame Home Package
Design, Budget, Estimate, and Secure Your Best Price

93

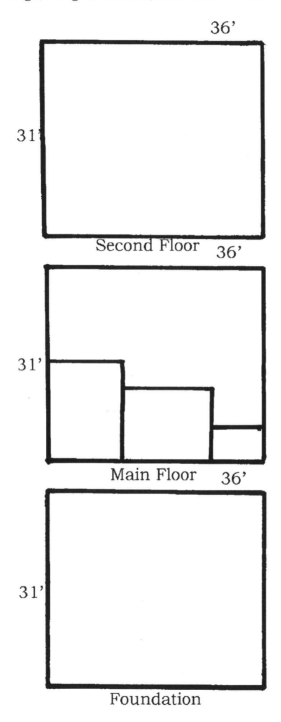

https://itunes.apple.com/ca/app/timber-frame-home-estimator/id901984861?mt=8

At this point your team's recorder will find the dimensions of the closets on your 3 favorite plans. Then calculate the average size. Also be sure to review positives and negatives pertaining to this often forgotten, but very important area of the home. Give these details to your Designer and update your rapidly changing floor plan.

We will now refer to this area as the Master Suite. This encompasses your Master Bedroom, Master Bathroom, and Master Closets. This area is complete for now and we can move on to the next area of the home. Before we do this, let's go through and label each one of the rooms we have so far. This way we do not confuse our spaces as we move forward. Nice work so far on the design, let's keep the positive momentum going. After labeling your drawings, they should look like this.

Timber Frame Home Package
Design, Budget, Estimate, and Secure Your Best Price

https://itunes.apple.com/ca/app/timber-frame-home-estimator/id901984861?mt=8

Chapter 15

Kitchen

The kitchen of a home has become the focal point of many plans so we are going to work on the placement of this room next. We will use the same principles we used to locate and size the master.

For Example:

Tom and Eva's top 3 plans have kitchens that are 8'x21', 10'x17', and 12'x13'. Tom computes the short wall average of (8'+10'+12')/3= 10'. The long wall average is (21'+17'+13')/3= 17'. This calculation determines that their plan should have a 10'x17' kitchen.

Tom then lists all the corresponding positives and negatives. Both Eva and Tom liked big kitchens that were not hidden from the living area of the home. A large open kitchen was common in their answers. They decided to choose a wall for their kitchen with this in mind. Eva takes this information and reflects it on their plans. You can see them on the next page.

Timber Frame Home Package
Design, Budget, Estimate, and Secure Your Best Price

App:
https://itunes.apple.com/ca/app/timber-frame-home-estimator/id901984861?mt=8

Now your building team's recorder can compile the dimensions of the kitchen in your favorite 3 prints and place them along side the positive and negatives. Once this information is available it should be given to the designer to note on your sketches. At this point it is not important to worry about the placement of the refrigerator, stove, dishwasher, and sinks. We are only concerned with reserving a space for the kitchen during this basic design exercise.

Timber Frame Home Package
Design, Budget, Estimate, and Secure Your Best Price

Download the Timber Frame Estimator App:
https://itunes.apple.com/ca/app/timber-frame-home-estimator/id901984861?mt=8

Chapter 16

Living Room/Great Room

Your living room or great room will typically be a room that you spend large amounts of relaxation time in. Using a similar process we are going to work on the placement of this room next.

For Example:

Tom & Eva's Top 3 plans have a great room that is 10'x30', 16'x16', and 14'x21'. Using the average method the short wall works out to (10'+16'+14')/3= 13.33' rounded down to 13. The long wall is averaged to (30'+16'+21')/3= 22.33' which averages down to 22'. Tom calculates a 13'x22' great room is what Eva will sketch onto their plans.

Using the needs list he places this information along with the positives and negatives on a sheet of paper and gives it to Eva. They both liked a large open great room and utilizing the average method allowed them to have a size they both can agree on of 13'x22'. They look for open placement in the middle of the plan. Eva, acting as the designer, draws this onto the plan.

Timber Frame Home Package
Design, Budget, Estimate, and Secure Your Best Price

https://itunes.apple.com/ca/app/timber-frame-home-estimator/id901984861?mt=8

It is now time for your recorder to find the dimensions of your living room and create the average so size and list the negatives and positives. Write these down and allow the designer to show them on the prints.

Download the Timber Frame Estimator App:
https://itunes.apple.com/ca/app/timber-frame-home-estimator/id901984861?mt=8

Chapter 17

Dining Room

This portion of the home can be tricky. In today's modern timber frame home a kitchen's space will double as a dining area and sometimes a living area. Typically this space will be adjacent to the kitchen so that you do not have to walk through another room with food to reach your dining area or table. For this area of the home try to find a remaining area adjacent to your kitchen and draw the area for your dining room.

For example:

Tom & Eva's plans have a dining room that is 6'x9', 6'x16', and 8'x14'. The short wall average is (6'+6'+8')/3= 6.33' which rounds down to 6'. The long wall works out to (9'+16'+14')/3= 13'. The size of their dining room will be 6'x13'.

Tom also reviews the positives and negatives for any comments about dining areas. The only comment he finds is a negative about a small dining room. Since the kitchen and great room area around the prospective dining area is wide open they both feel comfortable with the placement below.

Take a look at the placement of their dining room on the following page:

Timber Frame Home Package
Design, Budget, Estimate, and Secure Your Best Price

105

https://itunes.apple.com/ca/app/timber-frame-home-estimator/id901984861?mt=8

Chapter 18

Half Bathroom

A half bath is typically located on the same floor as the Master Suite to keep visitors from having to use a bathroom that is located in or near your Master bedroom. We are going to place a half bath onto your floor plan.

For Example:

Tom and Eva have dimensions for main level baths in their plans of 8'x10', 8'x10', and 6'x7'. The short wall works out to (8'+8'+6')/3= 6.67' which rounds up to 7'. The long wall calculation looks like (10'+10'+7')/3= 9'. Tom finds an average of 7'x9' for their half bathroom.

He finds no comments about the half bath on their list of positives and negatives. Eva draws these onto to their floor plan that is now taking shape.

See their updated sketches on the next page.

Timber Frame Home Package
Design, Budget, Estimate, and Secure Your Best Price

107

https://itunes.apple.com/ca/app/timber-frame-home-estimator/id901984861?mt=8

Using the same processes your recorder can now create your half bathroom's average size and positive and negatives. The designer will reflect them onto the prints.

Download the Timber Frame Estimator App:
https://itunes.apple.com/ca/app/timber-frame-home-estimator/id901984861?mt=8

Chapter 19

Stairs

If you have a second floor or basement you are also going to need a way to access it. In a smaller home a set of stairs can take up a large portion of the floor plan. However, they must be there. One solution in a timber frame home is to have the timber frame company provide a set of heavy timber stairs that are visually pleasing. They look less like an intrusion and more like a well thought out architectural detail.

We are going to place the stairs where both ends can be accessed. In addition the stair dimensions will be placed on all three floors in the exact same location.

For example:

Tom & Eva's plan has a space that looks almost perfect for a set of stairs. To see if they will fit we will calculate the average. The first plans had staircases that were 4'x15', 4'x15', and 4'x15'. It can easily be determined that the average staircase size is 4'x15'. There were no comments about the stairs in the positives and negatives section so Tom gives Eva the information. He also reminds her that the same set of stairs must be shown on all three floors.

You can see their drawings of the stairs on all three levels on the following page.

Download the Timber Frame Estimator App:
https://itunes.apple.com/ca/app/timber-frame-home-estimator/id901984861?mt=8

Chapter 20

Foundation

For the foundation page, if you have any finished area we will undertake the same exercises. The most common basement rooms are man caves, wine cellars, laundry rooms, utility rooms, and storage areas. Also there are many more uses that you may have already delegated your finished foundation space for.

Just be sure to stick to your completion percentage from the blind budget worksheet. The recorders should review information from the need assessment. This will provide a percentage of the basement that will be fully finished.

For Example:

Tom's worksheet showed that he would like to finish 75% of the basement and Eva wants to finish only 50%. They agree to take an average and finish out 62.5% of the basement. This will give them an additional 625 square feet to place their laundry room, utility room, storage closets, and a workshop. The 37.5% area that will not be finished will be left open for now.

The plans they chose only show a utility room. To keep the progress going Tom and Eva decide to place the utility room according to the average method. They will then use the same size room to accommodate a laundry

Download the Timber Frame Estimator App:
https://itunes.apple.com/ca/app/timber-frame-home-estimator/id901984861?mt=8

room, and a room that doubles as storage and a workshop.

The room in their plans measures 12'x12', 8'x25', and 11'x12'. The short wall averages (12'+8'+11')/3= 10.33' and rounds down to 10'. The long wall average is (12'+25'+12')/3 and averages 16.33'. This averages down to 16'. Therefore they will place 3 rooms in the foundation that are 10'x16'.

Timber Frame Home Package
Design, Budget, Estimate, and Secure Your Best Price

https://itunes.apple.com/ca/app/timber-frame-home-estimator/id901984861?mt=8

If you have any finished area in your foundation go ahead and create your rough layout. Use the same process as we used for the main floor and do not utilize any of the area that you agreed not to use in the worksheet chapter of the book. After the home is complete, and you are under your budget, this may be an area to spend your emergency building budget. As of right now it is strictly off limits for both design and additional rooms.

Chapter 21

Second Floor

Depending on your design the second floor may be just as design intensive as your first floor. Several bedrooms, baths, and additional family rooms may need to be placed on this level to make your home complete. Follow the same steps we took for your main level and let averages, your needs, and your favorite plans guide you as you move through the process.

For Example:

The worksheets Tom and Eva Created earlier showed that they would have anywhere from 60%-80% of their floor plan opened to the main floor as a loft. This means that the usable loft could range in size from 200-400 square feet. The Recorder reviewed the budget on this item and since they have a high budget number of $27,000 for this area they have decided to go with the smaller square footage of 200 to make sure that stay within their budget. They then go through and take the average of their favorite three plans lofts and their dimensions are 10'x24', 10'x25', and 12'x20'. The short side of the loft will average to (10'+10'+12')/3= 10.67'. This rounds up to 11'. The long side of the loft would average to (24'+25'+20')/3= 23'. This means the loft will be 10'x23'.

Download the Timber Frame Estimator App:
https://itunes.apple.com/ca/app/timber-frame-home-estimator/id901984861?mt=8

Tom also details the positives and negatives that were mentioned about their favorite plans. Among them they know they will need an upstairs bath. This will be addressed in the next section. They also wanted to guard against their loft being too small. Tom notates this information and the ideal size. He then passes the information on to Eva. She reflects the information on their Second Floor Plan.

You can see the plan Tom and Eva sketched on the next page that now includes the second floor.

Timber Frame Home Package
Design, Budget, Estimate, and Secure Your Best Price

https://itunes.apple.com/ca/app/timber-frame-home-estimator/id901984861?mt=8

Follow the same steps with your second floor make sure any issues or disagreements are settled by using the needs assessment, budget, and worksheets you created earlier. A process like the one we underwent in creating the main floor may be necessary depending on the amount of square footage you have on your second floor. Hopefully at this point you are comfortable with your roles and can operate smoothly as a team in creating your prints.

Chapter 22

Second Floor Bathroom

There may also be a need for an additional bathroom on the second floor. It will be up to you to decide whether this will be a half bath or a full bath.

For Example:

Chapter 23

Windows and Doors

For this portion of the home we are going to undertake a similar group design exercise. Make two copies of your prints and give one to the designer and the recorder. Each of you should make one floor plan with your desired window and door openings. Keep it simple and take a moment to sketch in the following:

1. Interior door locations
2. Exterior door locations
3. Exterior window locations
4. Eliminate unneeded interior walls

In Tom and Eva's example they draw in the following:

Download the Timber Frame Estimator App:
https://itunes.apple.com/ca/app/timber-frame-home-estimator/id901984861?mt=8

Tom's Opening Plan

Timber Frame Home Package
Design, Budget, Estimate, and Secure Your Best Price

125

Eva's Opening Plan

Download the Timber Frame Estimator App:
https://itunes.apple.com/ca/app/timber-frame-home-estimator/id901984861?mt=8

Now the designer and recorder on your team should take their copies of the sketches and go work in private. They will draw in the four items above and update the plans as much as possible.

Once these items are complete the team members will come back together and discuss each other's placement according to needs, positives, negatives, and the reasoning behind the placements. The recorder will make a note of which items are agreed upon. The designer will take these items and reflect the team's wishes onto the extra blank copy.

In Tom and Eva's example the windows and doors they placed in identical locations are on the next page:

Timber Frame Home Package
Design, Budget, Estimate, and Secure Your Best Price

127

Download the Timber Frame Estimator App:
https://itunes.apple.com/ca/app/timber-frame-home-estimator/id901984861?mt=8

After noting the windows and doors they agreed upon, there were still a few openings that needed to be added. They still needed a connection from the master bedroom to the master bathroom. They also both wanted another window in the kitchen. As a final compromise they agreed that a window in the dining room would be a nice additional touch for added natural light.

You can see their plan showing the three windows they added as part of their compromise alongside their initial openings on the next page:

Timber Frame Home Package
Design, Budget, Estimate, and Secure Your Best Price

129

https://itunes.apple.com/ca/app/timber-frame-home-estimator/id901984861?mt=8

After window and door opening sketches are complete go ahead and date them. All team members can initial the pages in the bottom right corner indicating their approval thus far. You will want to make 4 copies of each page.

The original sketch you will probably want to hold onto and frame. Then you can look back on your first design, after your home is complete. For your records you might also want to keep a well-used copy of this book to remind you of how you created your design.

Your next blank copy of the plans is going to act as your master copy. The Recorder will store it in the notebook without any further alterations. The other two copies will be personal copies for the Recorder and the Designer. The final copy is the one that you will mesh together as a team if any design alterations take place during the timber frame home package quoting process.

After this is complete, you can give yourselves a pat on the back. The hardest part of the process is now complete. For the exterior of the plan, or the elevations, I am going to ask you to hold off for now. Any clippings from magazines, pictures, and elevations you find desirable will be helpful for your recorder to compile in a notebook. Hold onto them for now, because even after 10 years in the industry drawing an elevation can prove difficult. For your preliminary design needs, a floor plan, a collection of information, and ideas about how you would like your exterior to look will prove just as valuable.

You have created a solid start for your timber frame home project and without spending more than $10.00 you designed a plan that includes all the essential steps I detailed. You have a solid budget, know what you need, you understand the land you will build on, and you have a design that you both have worked hard to create.

Most importantly you opened the lines of communication with your building partner and proved that you can work together and respect each team member's designs and ideas. With this viable preliminary design and a solid team structure in place, we can now move forward to working with a timber frame company.

Download the Timber Frame Estimator App:
https://itunes.apple.com/ca/app/timber-frame-home-estimator/id901984861?mt=8

Chapter 24

Timber frame Home Company

Now the recorder and designer have become a solid team, and the project is off on the right foot. It is time to interview the next real professional on the job, the timber frame home project manager.

Many people may argue at this step you should already know whom you would use as your general contractor. My reasoning for having you hold off is that your project manager may have ideas as to who is best suited to be your general contractor due to projects they have completed in the past. Also they may provide different levels of services and systems that could make having a general contractor with timber frame home experience more or less important.

For Example:

Timber frame Company A

Timber frame Company "A" pre-cuts all the timbers, installs pre-cut wiring chases, and provides detailed blueprints. They also offer unlimited no-cost technical assistance coupled with in-house timber installation crew that will install all of your structural timbers according to the industry's best standards.

Download the Timber Frame Estimator App:
https://itunes.apple.com/ca/app/timber-frame-home-estimator/id901984861?mt=8

Imagine you have hired this timber frame company to design your timber frame system, manufacture, and install your timbers. Now a general contractor who only specializes in heavy timber homes may not be as important. The contractor can spend more of their time focusing on regular general contractor duties like managing subcontractors for electrical, plumbing, framing and finishes.

The next example:

Timber frame Company B

Timber frame Company "B" does not pre-cut any of the timbers and only delivers rough lengths of timbers. These packs of long length timbers are sent to the site. Once on site the general contractor is now in charge of installing the timbers, cutting out windows and doors, drilling for wiring chases, and cutting notches and joinery on-site.

In this instance a general contractor with maximum timber frame home experience is essential, because he not only is responsible for managing subs, but also must insure that timbers are cut on-site according to acceptable building practices and your plans.

In the example the cost of a pre-cut package from Timber frame Company "A" will typically be higher than that of a package that is sent in rough lengths. Just imagine for a moment that when you bought your 5 year old a Lego set to open on Christmas morning you had similar options. On the shelf at the big box store were two sets of Lego's to build the same block castle shown on the front of the box.

The first set of building blocks would correspond directly to a set of step-by-step instructions. Block number 1 would be the exact size it needed to be and is placed in a specified location per the instructions. The same would be true for the blocks numbered 2 through 100, as the castle was constructed and completed.

The second set of Lego's for the exact same castle shows the same exact castle on the front of the box. When you brought the box home and opened the package the box would only contain 10 Lego blocks. Each of these blocks would be 10' long. It would now be your job to take these 10' Lego blocks, setup a suitable saw for ABS plastic and cut them down to a usable size that corresponds to what will be need for blocks 1 through 100.

In this instance the Lego set number 1 would have a higher initial price tag at the retailer because the manufacturer has taken the time to cut the blocks for you, number them, and make sure they fit together. They will slide together smoothly and by dinner on Christmas Day on your living room floor there would be a completed Lego castle. If a block somehow came in the Lego box that was the wrong size, or missing all together, a simple call to the company could have a replacement block on the way to you with minimal delays. For the second block castle the initial cost from the big box store will be lower. However the on-site labor demands, equipment needs, and cost could quickly meet and exceed the total cost of the first set of building blocks.

Download the Timber Frame Estimator App:
https://itunes.apple.com/ca/app/timber-frame-home-estimator/id901984861?mt=8

After unpacking your 10-foot long Lego blocks on the living room floor Christmas morning, you must then set up a plastic saw and find the specifications for Block 1. You cut block 1 and install it according to the instructions then repeat with blocks 2 through 100. Imagine you read the specifications wrong, saw at the wrong angle, or damage a block with a dull saw blade. It may be possible for you to re-use it in another location. If not, you must then call the block company and re-order another 10-foot block length, or install a defective block into the castle's wall. Then hope the less than quality Lego construction practice has no later ramifications.

This block castle that is started on Christmas morning may take until Valentine's Day to complete and be of lesser quality when finished. The initial cost of the packages are now becoming very similar, and the cost of becoming an on-site plastic block expert will probably cost more than allowing the experts at the Lego factory to pre-cut your block castle. Not to mention your 5 year old lost interest by New Year's Eve and is now playing with Ninja Turtles.

When choosing your timber frame home company there are several items to consider. I have broken these criteria down to the five most important questions and put them in a checklist much like we used in the previous chapters. You can satisfy these checklists with a call to different timber frame home companies.

Chapter 25

Timber frame Styles and Profiles

There are many different timber frame styles. By now you may or may not know the style of timber frame that suits you the best. You might however know which style you find the most aesthetically pleasing. Before placing a call to a timber frame home company you need to take the time necessary to add a specific timber frame style to your list of needs.

It is possible that along the path you will find a system that is better suited to you, more structurally sound, or appeals to you more. It is ok to price two separate systems with one timber frame home company. You must continue to adhere to your list of needs, budget, and the criteria in your timber frame company checklist. If a timber frame home company does not offer your specific timber frame style then cross them off the list.

Download the Timber Frame Estimator App:
https://itunes.apple.com/ca/app/timber-frame-home-estimator/id901984861?mt=8

Chapter 26

How long has the Timber frame Home Company been in business?

Timber frame homes and the way they are designed, built, and sold have undergone many changes over the past 200 years. Now take a look at the technological advances in insulation, anchoring systems, fasteners, blueprints, wiring chases, and the many little things that an untrained eye never sees. These all make up timber frame home system. Then you begin to realize that the only remaining similarities between a 200 year old timber frame cabin and today's technological masterpieces are the timber frames themselves.

When choosing a timber frame company, I must recommend that you choose a timber frame home company that has been a part of creating these advancements. Practice makes perfect, but you do not want to be a part of timber frame home company's practice. You want your home to be an example of their perfect. This is why I recommend that your criteria for a timber frame home company be that they have been manufacturing and installing timber frame home packages for at

Download the Timber Frame Estimator App:
https://itunes.apple.com/ca/app/timber-frame-home-estimator/id901984861?mt=8

least 35 years. The reason why is best shown in an example of the car industry.

There are new car companies that pop up every so often then fade into oblivion. They make a new car style that will supposedly be the next big thing. Then the trend fails to stick. After hearing about them on the nightly news for a few months you never hear another word mentioned. The same is very true of the timber frame home industry.

Noise is created by the new car companies in the press, but you continue driving your Chevrolet, Ford, Dodge, Honda, Toyota, BMW, or Toyota. Why? These companies pioneered the industry and the technology that has advanced it. Plus they proved they could make reliable products, survived industry downfalls, and have ultimately built products that met their customer's needs over the long term.

A new timber frame home company may still be perfecting their Model T. I doubt that anyone smart enough to read this book has ever taken a risk on a Tesla, Tango, SABO, Wheego, or Tata automobile. Nor would they put their child in one on their 16th birthday. No doubt some of these companies will withstand the test of time. What if they do not? Will it be the unproven brand of car you chose to take a chance on?

In ten years when you need a basic part can you call them and have the part shipped from the factory if they are out of business? If you did find the part would it be at a reasonable price? Or would you have to improvise or sell the car at a loss and chalk it up to a lesson learned?

Timber Frame Home Package
Design, Budget, Estimate, and Secure Your Best Price

The value of a timber frame company with a long tradition is very similar to the car industry. After market parts will never cease to exist. There are previous customers who can share their experiences. A company with long-standing expertise is not just testing their Model T of timber frame cabins on you. They have long since perfected the safety, quality, service, and installation of their homes.

Finally any 35-year-old timber frame company has survived a recession in the early 1980's and the most recent one as well. If managing money on the project is important to you, and I know it is. This means hiring a well-aged timber frame home company with a long track record of financial stability. A 35-year operational threshold is the minimum for a timber frame home company you will bring onto your project and this will be one of your uncompromising requirements. The next chapter sheds more light on the issue.

Download the Timber Frame Estimator App:
https://itunes.apple.com/ca/app/timber-frame-home-estimator/id901984861?mt=8

Chapter 27

Has your timber frame home company suffered a recent bankruptcy?

We have not reviewed the deposits required to start your timber frame home package yet, but trust me, we will. How would it make you feel if you knew that the timber frame home company you were about to write a large check to had just suffered a recent bankruptcy?

This was going to be my easiest criteria to help you make your pick of companies. I was going to tell you to take your top companies, enter them into a Google search bar. Then type the word "bankruptcy" behind it. An example would be, "Timber frame Company A Bankruptcy." Since bankruptcies are typically public records it is harder and harder for any company that fails to live up to their financial obligations to hide from the fact that they publicly requested relief.

As a form of research for this book, I got online and practiced with a few. Most came out clean as a whistle. Then I practiced with the company with whom I had over a decade of experience with, Hearthstone Homes. Instantly 9 pages of information on Hearthstone Homes bankruptcy popped onto the screen. This would be a deal breaker for anyone of my readers.

However, I was certain this was not the same Hearthstone Homes from Dandridge, TN that I worked for. I knew this because I had been in the corporate office over the past decade and know their financial positions. It turned out that the defunct Hearthstone Homes was a similarly named large-scale conventional builder from Omaha, Nebraska. This was not Hearthstone Log and Timberframe Homes from Dandridge, TN.

In this day and age of instant eye tests using the Internet, I would have disqualified a quality manufacturer based on bad information. I am also certain Hearthstone has probably lost some business in the past due to this very issue. There is nothing a company can do when an unconnected business halfway across the country shares a name. Then the similarly named company has financial difficulties.

As part of my research for this book I had stumbled upon information that brought to light why I had received calls from prospective clients asking about Hearthstone's Nebraska office. I always thought it was weird, because we did not have one. Now I understand why.

As part of your bankruptcy research I would caution you to investigate the links you find thoroughly and disqualify any company only based on a confirmed link and bankruptcy. After all, there are dozens of companies with Dream, River, Works, Crafter,

Frame, Timber, and Mill in their names. You might exclude a well-qualified, financially stable company, with the best product available, by giving search results a quick eye test. I almost did.

In the timber frame home industry we are never proud when a competitor goes bankrupt. It gives the entire industry a black eye. When clients lose deposits, projects do not ship, and customers lose confidence in the industry overall, it hurts everyone. In the most recent recession, it seemed like a daily occurrence.

Also beware that some of the companies that bankrupted are popping back up now as the economy improves. They do this re-incorporation either under their old name, or they branch out and create new companies with the same bankrupted company's employees. If you find a 35-year-old company in the industry and follow my advice about not writing checks to recently bankrupted corporations, or their employees, you would be wise.

If in your research you can positively conclude that a company has been bankrupt I would pass on their products and services. Over the years many companies have been unable to pay their bills and left clients stranded with tens of thousands of dollars in deposits. The timbers the client ordered will never arrive on site or be produced.

From the very beginning of this book you based your project on a foundation of a reasonable budget. Why would you ever trust your hard-earned money, and your timber

Download the Timber Frame Estimator App:
https://itunes.apple.com/ca/app/timber-frame-home-estimator/id901984861?mt=8

frame home package, to a company who cannot manage their own budget?

Chapter 28

Are the timbers pre-cut at the timber frame home factory?

If you remember my Lego example from earlier there are advantages to having timbers pre-cut by the timber frame home company. This is the exact reason why you cannot buy 10' Lego blocks to cut yourself. If you want to save time and money on your timber frame home project your timbers need to be cut by a company who has invested in equipment and personnel to cut your timber frames correctly.

The days of on site timberframes being made with a chainsaw are numbered. Rapidly advancing building codes and the high cost of building a home shabbily are all to blame. Also these poorly constructed timber frame cabins are a dying breed. This is because of smart people like you who choose to take the time to read this book before placing their deposit.

Download the Timber Frame Estimator App:
https://itunes.apple.com/ca/app/timber-frame-home-estimator/id901984861?mt=8

The pre-cut package will cost more upfront than a company that only sells lengths of timber frames from a mill. Your labor cost and the price of errors will quickly even this price difference out after the first 3 months on site, guaranteed. If the parts to build your timber frame cabin are going to be manufactured on your jobsite politely end your phone call and move onto the next timber frame home company on your list.

Chapter 29

Will your timber frame home company send a crew to install their own products?

A company that will install their own timber package on site is worth its weight in gold on a timber frame home project. A company that will not construct their own timber frame package does not have confidence in the quality of the products that they produce. They will not risk sending their own people to a site, because they know how tedious and labor intensive installing poorly manufactured timbers can be.

You must find a company that will install their timber frame system for you. A timber frame home company is only as good as their installation crews and having an inexperienced crew is a recipe for disaster. Why not take advantage of the many companies that offer fixed cost installation services of their own products? There is not a

Download the Timber Frame Estimator App:
https://itunes.apple.com/ca/app/timber-frame-home-estimator/id901984861?mt=8

single disadvantage, especially when it is coupled with an exceptional warranty.

If a company has enough confidence in the products that they will send it thousands of miles from their factory and install the timber frames with their own team this is whom you need on your project. They install it, because they know they have manufactured it correctly and this is whom you want to do business with.

The leaders in the industry will offer you a fixed cost estimate on labor. This will include a crew, the crane, and all the labor that it takes to offload and install their products at a fixed cost. This takes us back to step number one in this book and allows us to adhere to our budget. Having inexperienced laborers or contractors install a timber frame product they are unfamiliar with is a sure fire way to exceed your labor costs before you even get a roof on your project.

Chapter 30

Timber Frame Home Company Interviews

Now Take these five questions and get out there and ask them to your desired timber frame home companies. You can quickly narrow down further whom the next professional will be that you add to your timber frame home staff.

A great way to handle these interview calls is to put the call on speakerphone and have the Designer ask the questions. The Recorder can write down the responses. I suggest two calls to see if the answers differ the next time you speak to the company. Before asking any timber frame home company for a proposal. A handy list that can be printed from **www.Jobe.ws**. It is shown on the next page.

5 Qualifying Questions

Download the Timber Frame Estimator App:
https://itunes.apple.com/ca/app/timber-frame-home-estimator/id901984861?mt=8

Do you offer my desired timber frame profile?

How long has the Timber frame Home Company been in business?

Has your timber frame home company suffered a recent bankruptcy?

Are the timbers pre-cut at the timber frame home factory?

Will your timber frame home company send a crew to install their own products?

Are You Serious?

If the company you interviewed qualified according to the questions above, and you want to move to the front of their priority list you made a good start by reading this book. Here are some basic questions you can ask your prospective timber frame home companies and watch the attention for your project grow.

Can I see a proposal and purchase agreement for that floor plan?

If I made a down payment today when can you have my timbers ready for delivery and installation?

At what times during the project will you personally visit my site?

I have my plans, budget, and land in hand. What would be my next step with your company?

I read Timber Frame Home Package so I have a high level of understanding of the industry standards. How does your company differ from the explained standards?

Chapter 31

Timber Frame Home Package Proposals

The proposal for your timber home is based upon your sketches we created in the design session of this book. After narrowing down your choices, send the plans you created off to the companies that passed our test. You can e-mail, mail, fax, or make a factory visit if distance allows.

Go ahead and ask the companies to give you a proposal with the maximum amount of materials and services they can provide for your project, in the timber frame style of your choice. The materials, services, and costs will differ from each company. Comparing these quotes will allow you to know the exact cost of

Download the Timber Frame Estimator App:
https://itunes.apple.com/ca/app/timber-frame-home-estimator/id901984861?mt=8

certain items and where the major discrepancies may be.

After reviewing your plans most companies offer a 24-48 hour turn around on material and labor proposals. Some can quote for you instantly using timber frame home estimating software on their computer. Once you get all the proposals you need to compare them side by side. It is time to analyze the timber sizes, timber frame profiles, and timber treatments on an equal playing field. See the example below of how I compare proposals, and then use the blank proposal comparison form to do your own. You can print this form for free from **www.Jobe.ws.**

Timber Frame Proposal Analysis

Blue Prints	Yes	No
Usable Square Footage	_____	
Wood Species	_____	
Rafter Size	_____	
Post Size	_____	
Maximum Timber length	_____	
Timber frame bent profiles		_____
Floor Beam Size	_____	
Girder Size	_____	

Timber Frame Home Package
Design, Budget, Estimate, and Secure Your Best Price

Pre-cut Structural Insulated Panels	Yes	No
Pre-cut electrical wiring chases	Yes	No
Kiln Dried Timbers	Yes	No
Loft Tounge & Groove Decking	Yes	No
Porch T&G Roof Decking	Yes	No
Interior T&G Roof Decking	Yes	No
Heavy Timber Stairs	Yes	No
Hand Hewn	Yes	No
Wall insulation	Yes	No
Caulking	Yes	No
Exterior stain	Yes	No
Interior stain	Yes	No
Siding	Yes	No
Lags & Screws	Yes	No
Porch System	Yes	No
Note Timber Sizes for Posts, Girders Rafters Plates		
Post Jacks	Yes	No

Download the Timber Frame Estimator App:
https://itunes.apple.com/ca/app/timber-frame-home-estimator/id901984861?mt=8

Oly Screws	Yes	No
Finish siding for Gable End	Yes	No
Roof Insulation Yes No R-value? ____		
Plywood for Gables	Yes	No
Plywood for Roof	Yes	No
Plywood for Shed Dormers	Yes	No
Plywood for Gable Dormers	Yes	No
Plywood for Porch Roof	Yes	No
Gable end framing lumber	Yes	No
Roofing Felt	Yes	No
Borate Powder	Yes	No
Felt Buttons	Yes	No
Shingles or Metal	Yes	No
Windows	Yes	No
Exterior Doors	Yes	No
Interior Doors	Yes	No
Freight	Yes	No
Material Offloaded upon delivery Yes No		

Other items:

Timber Frame Home Package
Design, Budget, Estimate, and Secure Your Best Price

Total Material Package Cost:

Sales Tax:

Total Material Cost:

Timber Installation   Yes   No

If yes, what is installed?

Dry In installation   Yes   No

If yes, what is installed?

    Now take one of these forms and work through it for each proposal so you can see what each proposal contains and lacks. You can print additional forms free of charge at my website **www.Jobe.ws**
    It is very possible that some of the proposals contain items that you will not need. For example if you wanted vinyl siding on your gable ends then you may not need the wood siding that several of the companies may have included. If your timber frame home companies have quoted unneeded items ask them to delete these materials from their package. Then go through and complete the previous worksheet once more.

Download the Timber Frame Estimator App:
https://itunes.apple.com/ca/app/timber-frame-home-estimator/id901984861?mt=8

Chapter 32

How I Might Be Able To Help

If the proposal analysis process seems tedious or you are feeling overwhelmed I have created some basic services. These are affordable, fast, and I can save you thousands of dollars on your project by using an insider with a decade of experience and knowledge to analyze your project and proposals.

Two Company Comparisons

Download the Timber Frame Estimator App:
https://itunes.apple.com/ca/app/timber-frame-home-estimator/id901984861?mt=8

Email or mail me your sketch, your basic needs, and your top two proposals. I will analyze your timber frame home company proposals and send you back a side-by-side comparison. This includes a list of five customized questions for each proposal to help you narrow down which company you should use. The cost for this service is a $99 consulting fee with results returned to you within 48 hours of payment, plan, needs, and proposal receipt.

Three Company Comparisons

Email or mail me your sketch, your basic needs, and your top three proposals. I will analyze your timber frame home company proposals and send you back a side-by-side comparison. This includes a list of five customized questions for each proposal to help you narrow down which company you should use. The cost for this service is a $149 consulting fee with results returned to you within 48 hours of payment, plan, needs, and proposal receipt.

Two Company Personal Project Assistant

E-mail me or mail me two proposals. I will analyze the proposals and compare them side-by-side. I will then call and ask the 5 customized questions for each proposal to the timber frame home companies you chose. Then I will relay the information back to you in the form of a written report followed by a personal phone call and assessment of your project. The cost for this service is a $199 consultation fee with results returned to you within 48 hours of payment, plan, needs, and proposal receipt.

Three Company Personal Project Assistant

E-mail me or mail me three proposals. I will analyze the proposals and compare them side-by-side. I will then call and ask the 5 customized questions for each proposal to the timber frame home companies you chose. Then I will relay the information back to you in the form of a written report followed by a personal phone call and assessment of your project. The cost for this service is a $249 consultation fee with results returned to you within 48 hours of payment, plan, needs, and proposal receipt.

Two Company Personal Negotiator

I will conduct an initial interview with you. During this interview I will analyze your budget, needs, plans, and proposals. I will contact your two top timber frame home companies and negotiate the best price and material package with each company. Then I will return a report to you along with a recommendation on which company would be the best to choose. The cost for this service is a consultation fee of $299.

Three Company Personal Negotiator

I will conduct an initial interview with you. During this interview I will analyze your

Download the Timber Frame Estimator App:
https://itunes.apple.com/ca/app/timber-frame-home-estimator/id901984861?mt=8

budget, needs, plans, and proposals. I will contact your three top timber frame home companies and negotiate the best price and material package with each company. Then I will return a report to you along with a recommendation on which company would be the best to choose. The cost of this service is a consultation fee of $349.

Package Energy Code Compliance

Does your package meet the codes of your local building department in regards to energy efficiency? Why would you purchase a package that does not? I will run a nationally recognized Residential Energy Check for your home, plan, and proposal. This will allow you to see beforehand if your insulation values are adequate. A minimum requirement for anyone wanting to buy a package that meets their needs. Send your jobsite location, plan, and proposal. $99 per company proposal.

My contact information for sending your information and ordering the above services is below. Feel free to ask any questions you may have about the services in a form of an email or letter.

E-mail: **JobeLeonard@gmail.com**

Mailing Address: Jobe Leonard
1511 Mayflower Lane
Dandridge, TN 37725

Do not feel like you have to use the services, as many of my readers are already perfectly capable of vetting the timber frame home companies themselves. This is a service I can provide at an extremely low cost and help a large number of people with the knowledge I have acquired in the industry over the past decade.

Chapter 33

Life after the proposal

So at this point you have chosen your proposal, and you know which company you will do business with. It is now time to enter into a contractual agreement. The industry standard is a 10% to 25% down payment on materials. Then 50% of the package price will be due to secure your delivery date.

Download the Timber Frame Estimator App:
https://itunes.apple.com/ca/app/timber-frame-home-estimator/id901984861?mt=8

A lower down payment is not always better because it inflates the size of your progress payments. This can make your next payment much more daunting. Final payments are typically due upon delivery, but may be negotiable. Do not be afraid to ask if a larger down payment of 50% to 75% could garner a significant discount. If I do your negotiating I will ask questions like this.

Timber frame home companies are unique because they incur 100% of the project's material expenses before they deliver the timber frame system. Cash is always king in the timber frame home industry. A great way to secure some additional savings is to beef up your down payment.

Most timber frame home companies have seen hundreds of client's walk away from 5% or 10% down payments. You will ease the manufacturer's mind by guaranteeing your project will ship by placing a larger down payment. This allows you to reduce their risk of order cancellation and therefore should decrease the overall cost of your timber frame home package.

Many people will say that a large down payment is never a good idea in the construction industry. I would disagree in this instance because we have already chosen companies that have 35+ years of experience, no financial trouble, erect their own products, and have a proven track record. If you have chosen to ignore some of my criteria for choosing a timber frame home company then I would tend to agree. I would then hesitate to give any deposit at all, let alone a 50%-75% "rainmaker".

You have your proposal settled and you have chosen your timber frame home project manager and the company you will do business with. You also have an agreement in hand to purchase your timber frame home package and installation services. This will get your construction blueprints started. Your timber frame home project manager is asking you on a daily basis to send in the agreement to get started. If you are comfortable with your investigation then go ahead and turn in the paperwork. If you want one last boost of confidence I can review it for you. If not, pull the trigger, you have done enough research on your own. It is now time to move forward.

Chapter 34

Your Contractor

You now need to find a contractor. This can take place while your timber frame home company is completing your initial set of blueprints. This can commonly take 4-6

Download the Timber Frame Estimator App:
https://itunes.apple.com/ca/app/timber-frame-home-estimator/id901984861?mt=8

weeks to create the first set of blueprints. These plans will be unique and are drawn site specific to where your project will deliver.

This gives you an acceptable amount of time to find a general contractor. Depending on the services your timber frame home company is providing your contractor will be responsible for each item that the timber frame home company does not install. Finding a good contractor can make or break your project. I am going to help you locate one.

You are going to begin another investigation. You will choose contractors to interview for your project. Here are some of the best sources for contractors.

-Family, Friends, Business Acquaintances
-Local Building Departments
-Realtors
-Lumberyards
-Ongoing projects in the area
-Your Timber frame Home Company

Ask all of these resources who they recommend if they were going to build a house. Stop by projects of similar construction in your area and ask to speak with the general contractor. After you have a solid list of general contractors it is now time to conduct interviews.

Try to think back to the last time you interviewed for a job. You cleaned up, polished your resume, and arrived 15 minutes early. While a builder may not put on a suit and tie, a contractor's resume is their previous projects. His references are current customers, former clients, subcontractors, and material suppliers. You are now going to be on the other side of the job interview process.

Minimum Requirements

Here is what you need the contractor to provide as minimum qualifications.

1. Worker's compensation and liability insurance
2. Copy of contractor's license
3. At least 3 references
4. Acceptable billing and accounting practices
5. Years of experience
6. Construction warranty

To further whittle down which builder you will use, consider these important traits that a contractor should possess. Use your interview process to gauge their suitability.

Traits you want....

1. Communication skills
2. Enthusiasm for your project
3. Teamwork
4. Budget Control

Traits you don't want....

Download the Timber Frame Estimator App:
https://itunes.apple.com/ca/app/timber-frame-home-estimator/id901984861?mt=8

1. Negative comments, feelings, or experiences with timber frame homes.
2. Know it all mentality
3. Arrogance
4. Scatter brain

Chapter 35

Moving Forward

4-6 weeks have passed, and your construction blueprints are complete. You

Download the Timber Frame Estimator App:
https://itunes.apple.com/ca/app/timber-frame-home-estimator/id901984861?mt=8

have conducted your initial interviews with contractor candidates. Now you will need to request at least 5 sets of blueprints from your timber frame home project manager, before they are sent.

Send each of your top contractors who passed the first round of interviews a set of your plans and a copy of what materials and services the timber frame home company will provide for the project. Remove the pricing then thoroughly explain what your chosen timber frame home company will handle. A conference call or meeting between the timber frame home project manager, the contractor, and you may be necessary.

Also at this point it is good to be aware of a contractor who feels threatened by the timber frame home company's kit or package. It is true that the timber frame home company will provide a large portion of the materials and services. This was your choice based on thorough research, your needs, and your budget. The moment a contractor tries to remove materials or services you have decided on is the moment you need to become suspect that the contractor is after a larger paycheck.

Some contractors can be a timber frame home project's best friend, and others can try to trim your package down to bare bones until there is barely a real timber in the entire home. Any effort to remove timbers or installation from the services you and your timber frame home company will provide should be seen as an early sign of inflexibility.

This could be the beginning of an overall effort to cheapen the quality of your project. You prepared the budget, design, picked the company, and narrowed down your list of contractors. There is a time to relinquish some control of your timber frame home project and give the contractor some creative freedoms, but it is not now.

Provide the remaining contractors with plans, a list of materials, and installation services. Ask them to provide you with a written proposal for the rest of the project. Use this as your final compliance test when making your decision on contractors.

Finally, after reviewing quotes from your top contractors it is time to evaluate each of the bids side by side. The cheapest bid is not always the best. If red flags pop up on any proposal it is your job to highlight and discuss them before signing any agreements.

Now that you have reviewed the construction proposals, they meet your needs, and the numbers are within your budget it is time to enter into an agreement with your general contractor. I suggest spending a little extra money to review the construction contract with a lawyer who is local to the job site. You can do this with or without the contractor's knowledge. Just have your legal counsel review the agreement and redline anything he is uncomfortable with and make some suggestions for suitable changes.

Then meet with your contractor and discuss your changes to the agreement and your concerns. Let him know you are ready to begin if your concerns can be met. At the point the contract is executed you may be responsible for a payment or retainer, but be sure to review these contract specifics before attending the meeting. If you are working

Download the Timber Frame Estimator App:
https://itunes.apple.com/ca/app/timber-frame-home-estimator/id901984861?mt=8

with a bank or a lending institution within the confines of a construction loan they will generally have rules regarding initial deposit amounts. Make sure this amount is suitable for the project you are undertaking. If the sum the bank will give is less than the contractor requires this may have to be another area for compromise.

Just like when you are buying a car, negotiating is extremely common when contracting to build a home. The only way you lose is if you do not try. The only bad situation that can happen is that the contractor says, "No."

Again this could indicate a sign of inflexibility that could derail the project later. Also it could mean the contractor might not possess the negotiating skills that are necessary to make your project a success.

Now that you have signed your agreement with the contractor, it is time to finalize your design. Sit down with your chosen contractor and mark any changes on the actual set of prints in red ink. Once this is complete, send the plans back to your timber frame home company.

This round of changes should take less time unless you make major changes to the structural systems, timbers, footprint, or layout. I would recommend using this final design session to tweak small details. Be careful when re-inventing the wheel at this late in the game. It could lead to a dreaded case of "designers disease." This is an illness where you lose sleep and constantly change details back and forth until your design services eat a large hole into your budget. This book and the design work that we undertook in the early phases should act as a great vaccination against this project-crippling ailment.

Plus you already have a proposal from your contractor based on your blueprints that you both agreed upon. This plan should already meet your needs, budget, and all the other major criteria we have discussed in this book. Keep the end target stationary because in building and in life, it is much harder to hit a moving target.

While you are waiting on your final set of blueprints your contractor can be moving ahead with site work. The initial steps can be taken care of with your preliminary plans as long as no major changes have been made to your layout, foundation, footprint, bedrooms, bathrooms, or structural details. If you have modified these parts, then you will need to wait for your final set of plans before you begin.

If you have not, your contractor can visit the local building inspector to begin the process for permits. Depending on your area this could range from a rubber stamp to full engineering. You should already know what to expect because of previous research. So there should be no surprises.

After pulling the permits, it is time to begin your site work. A driveway is needed to get materials to the site. This pathway should be graveled, but unpaved until the project is 99% complete. This will prevent you from having to repave it from heavy construction equipment damage. Next the contractor will work on details for the septic, electric, and

Download the Timber Frame Estimator App:
https://itunes.apple.com/ca/app/timber-frame-home-estimator/id901984861?mt=8

water systems. Then they begin to excavate for the foundation.

As final plans arrive the contractor can now begin to work on the footers according to final plans. Never start or allow your contractor to work on any part of the foundation for a timber frame home until your final prints are in hand. One inch of variation can make for a very expensive problem when it comes to timber frames. Timber frame home companies have advanced the technological capabilities greatly over the past 200 years. However, the industry has not been able to create a timber frame stretcher to make short timber frames longer. That is, as of the date of this book's publication.

Your final plans arrive. They meet your needs, and it is now time to send your timber frame home company a set of signed finals and any agreed upon progress payment to satisfy your previous agreements. This should also be when you will lock in your delivery day with the timber frame home company and contractor. Request the delivery day in writing before sending the plans or the check so you can maintain leverage. Then hold everyone involved to his or her agreements, including yourself.

You may also request that your project manager make one additional visit to your site to double-check your finished subfloor the week before delivery. If the foundation is wrong, the timber frames are still at the factory. You may have to pay extra to have the foundation fixed or the timber frames re-cut. At least you do not have to pay the price to have timber frames shipped to your site, back to the factory, then back to your site once more.

Now that your timber frame company and contractor know your plans are final and the timbers are set for delivery both your contractor and timber company will be working feverishly. The contractor is on site managing subcontractors for concrete, footers, foundation walls, plumbing, electrical, joists, and the subfloor. The timber frame home manufacturer is at their facility processing your timbers and reviewing your project with their installation crew. They make each piece of your timber frame home package according to your specifications. Then when it arrives on site it will fit like a pre-cut block in a Lego castle.

Chapter 36

Timber frame Delivery Day

Download the Timber Frame Estimator App:
https://itunes.apple.com/ca/app/timber-frame-home-estimator/id901984861?mt=8

If everything moves as planned, and your project manager gives you the thumbs up on the foundation, then both ends of the construction process will meet on your timber frame delivery day. Trucks from your timber frame home manufacturer will caravan onto the site with a crane and the installation crew. Final payments are made and the timber frame construction crew will offload the materials from the truck onto your site. Before setting the first timber the installation crew will double-check the foundation once more for dimensional integrity. Then the crews begin setting the timbers.

The typical timber frame installation crew for a 2,000 square foot home can dry in the structure in 7-14 days. This timeframe could fluctuate up or down due to weather, size of crew, expertise, or complexity of timberwork.

Ask your contractor to be on site to assist. Ask questions of the crew as they progress. Some of the most knowledgeable and friendly people that work for a timber frame home company are on the installation crews. They know heavy timber construction, because it is all they do. Consider bringing them lunch one day during the installation process as a gesture of good will. You just might find they alert you to any issues or help you out by handling an area of installation that was not on their work order. Maybe even doing this without an additional charge.

Your contractor can manage other subs while the crew is on site. They should also use the timber crews to gain first hand knowledge of the areas that they may have still questions about. He or she can acquire this information just by being on site and making himself available.

Now it is 7-14 days later and the timber frame installation crew is packing up to move onto their next timber frame installation job. They have completed the items on your agreement, and they clean up their trash before hitting the road.

A quality timber frame company, like the one you chose, will now offer an on-site walk through to discuss the project with you. If you or your contractor have any immediate concerns, then it is best to call your project manager. Make these concerns known before the crew leaves, and not an hour after they drive away. This way the cost for the timber frame home company to make amends is minimal. A reputable company will be happy to take care of any issues they have created or overlooked while they are still on site. A company built with service in mind will take care of it immediately, and that is who this book helped you ultimately choose.

If the crew is gone, then request a meeting with your project manager. Pictures of any issues are helpful and can allow identification of the issue from afar. Plus they act as documentation that the issue was present and you brought it to your project manager's attention. If the issue is minor, and you have confidence it will be handled, then pressing for an immediate meeting may not be needed. Use your gut on this and allow the timber frame company to exercise

Download the Timber Frame Estimator App:
https://itunes.apple.com/ca/app/timber-frame-home-estimator/id901984861?mt=8

any warranty or guarantee they offer before losing your cool.

If your calls go unanswered and your concerns are not met then escalating the complaint to the president or CEO of the timber frame home company is your next timber frameical step. You can do this through a phone call or written letter sent via registered mail.

Rest assured your issue will be handled. You have taken the time to choose a quality teammate, and the reason they are still in business today is because they know how to handle issues both big and small.

Many times as the project reaches the completion stages certain finishes that are only available from your original timber frame company are needed. It makes a lot of sense to use the same materials to tie the project together aesthetically. While sticking to your budget, do your best to place all these items into one order and call your timber frame company's project manager. Let them know you have a miscellaneous order and ask for any applicable repeat client discounts. Also offer to host an open house or to meet and tour any local clients in exchange for an additional price breaks.

Download the Timber Frame Estimator App:
https://itunes.apple.com/ca/app/timber-frame-home-estimator/id901984861?mt=8

Chapter 37

Completion

Now that all issues are settled and your contractor is on site every day managing your subcontractors your dream begins turning into reality. Day by day you see a finished roof going on followed by windows and doors.
Simultaneously the electrical, plumbing and HVAC contractors are working in concert to install their systems and you can finally see an end in sight. You pick your kitchen cabinets, countertops, finish flooring, and bathroom fixtures. Then your exterior porches are finished.
As the days progress stay away from making "small" changes by switching a room from carpet to wood and vinyl to stone. The cost of an individual change may be small, but they add up in the end and can cause your target budget to move upward. Stick as close as possible to what you agreed upon with your contractor. This way you can avoid surprises at the end of the project that might grab hold of your emergency budget.
You can now begin to plan that first Thanksgiving dinner, Christmas morning, or your fireplace's first fire on a crisp fall evening following summer's end.

Download the Timber Frame Estimator App:
https://itunes.apple.com/ca/app/timber-frame-home-estimator/id901984861?mt=8

About the author

Jobe Leonard lives in Dandridge, TN. After attending Tennessee Technological University he received his MBA at Lincoln Memorial University. He is a project manager with Hearthstone Homes and has currently built over 100 custom log and timber frame homes in 26 different states. This includes a recent project he managed that was named the 2012 National Log Home of the Year. In addition, he is the owner of LakeFun.com where he serves as the current CEO of this Internet startup company. He is also a writer, contributor, and content creator for GoOverseas.com. For more information on his current projects, other books, and free worksheets visit www.Jobe.ws.

If you enjoyed reading this guide I would appreciate your honest review on Amazon, Facebook, or Twitter. Also tell a friend and help me spread the word. Send any questions to JobeLeonard@gmail.com

Made in the USA
Middletown, DE
13 December 2018